I NEED THEE EVERY HOUR

Applying the Atonement in Everyday Life

OTHER BOOKS AND AUDIO BOOKS
BY DAVID P. VANDAGRIFF:

*Deliverance from Depression—Finding Hope and Healing Through
the Atonement of Christ*

I NEED THEE EVERY HOUR

Applying the Atonement in Everyday Life

DAVID P. VANDAGRIFF

Covenant Communications, Inc.

Cover image *Lord, I Believe* © 2010 Liz Lemon Swindle. Used with permission from Foundation Arts. For print information go to www.foundationarts.com or call 1.800.366.2781.

Cover design copyrighted 2010 by Covenant Communications, Inc.

Published by Covenant Communications, Inc.
American Fork, Utah

Printed in The United States of America
First Printing: February 2010

16 15 14 13 12 11 10   10 9 8 7 6 5 4 3 2 1

ISBN-13: 978-1-59811-910-7

This book is dedicated to my wife, G.G., who was the first Latter-day Saint I met and who began to share the gospel with me during our first conversation and has never stopped.

ACKNOWLEDGMENTS

I would like to thank Thomas B. Griffith, former president of the Brigham Young University Nineth Stake, for teaching me the central importance of the Atonement and asking that every talk and lesson in the stake be explicitly connected to the Atonement. His instruction changed my life.

My deep gratitude also goes to the dedicated and wonderful men who served as my counselors when I was a bishop—John Nummela, Kendon Eakett, Paul Ruffner, Ralph Yarro, Bill Maloy, Lane Nielson, William Bladh, and Robert Leavitt. Each was an example and an inspiration to me and showed me how a faithful priesthood leader magnifies his calling.

Finally, I would like to extend my sincere appreciation to the former members of the Pierce City, Missouri, and Brigham Young University 28th Wards, who taught me so much by precept and example while I had the privilege to serve as their bishop.

A STATEMENT ABOUT DOCTRINE

I have endeavored to conform every aspect of this book to the doctrines of The Church of Jesus Christ of Latter-day Saints. Any failure to do so is my error alone. If any part of this book conflicts with statements of Church authorities—past, present, or future—please regard those parts of my writing as erroneous and accept my apologies.

CONTENTS

INTRODUCTION

*We believe that through the Atonement
of Christ, all mankind may be saved, by obedience
to the laws and ordinances of the Gospel.*

—Article of Faith 1:3

*[The Atonement of Christ] is the very root of Christian
doctrine. You may know much about the gospel as it branches
out from there, but if you only know the branches and those branches
do not touch that root, if they have been cut free from that truth,
there will be no life nor substance nor redemption in them.*

—President Boyd K. Packer, "The Mediator," *Ensign*, May 1977, 56

*I need thee every hour,
In joy or pain,
Come quickly and abide,
Or life is vain.*

—"I Need Thee Every Hour," *Hymns*, no. 98

THE Atonement of Jesus Christ is not only for your last breath and the last day of your life, but it is also for every day of your life, every breath of your life. The Atonement is the most important event that ever has occurred or ever will occur at any time or in any place in our universe.

The Atonement is wonderful to think about on Sunday. When I had the privilege of being bishop of a Brigham Young University singles ward, I asked that every talk and every lesson be explicitly connected to the Atonement of Christ. In an Old Testament Sunday School class, the lesson could be Jonah and the Atonement. For a sacrament meeting, the assigned topic might be tithing and the Atonement. This principle—the Atonement—had a transforming effect on the members of that ward and their bishop. The spiritual afterglow of our Sunday services continued through the remainder of the day for me. But if the Atonement is important, refreshing, and uplifting on Sunday, it is at least equally so on every other day of the week. In our daily lives—every hour—as we encounter our small and large joys and challenges and as we strive to serve Christ by serving those around us, we need the Atonement.

When we are in a spiritual setting, surrounded by a group of Latter-day Saints who are striving to become a little better, those around us help to sustain, encourage, and reinforce our spiritual aspirations. Such a gathering invites the Spirit, and all present are uplifted in large and small ways that are personal to them. When we leave that gathering, walk out of church, and go back into the world, the sustaining influence of our fellow strivers may begin to fade. Monday comes and with it the challenges of living by the Spirit in a mortal world that is often hostile to spiritual aspirations.

But it is during the hours of our everyday life that we work out our salvation, usually unobserved by others, sometimes feeling alone and often feeling opposed. If we are to find success on such days, we need a Savior.

The necessity of a Savior came because of the Fall of Adam and Eve. Because of their transgression, they were cast out of the Garden of Eden, deprived of face-to-face association with God the Father and Jesus Christ. As children of Adam, we did not inherit his transgression, but we did inherit his circumstances. With bodies created from the elements of our fallen world, we need the Savior in order to live successfully in that world. We need His Atonement every second, every hour, and every day.

This book will share some ideas about applying the Atonement every hour and every day. Extending the principle that worked so well in my student ward, I'll talk about how we can link the Atonement with the sometimes mundane tasks comprising mortality. Applying the Atonement during the week is often harder than doing so on

Sunday. Combining temple worship and the Atonement is an easier undertaking than combining peeling potatoes and the Atonement or fixing the plumbing and the Atonement.

To explain how we can successfully combine the Atonement with our daily lives, I will use some experiences I have had as a bishop, once in a family ward and once in a student ward. Some may ask, "I'm never going to be a bishop. How can I identify with a bishop's experiences?" In answer, I'll just say that there are very few things that only a bishop can do. In retrospect, the most important acts I performed as a bishop were to mourn with those who mourned; comfort those who stood in need of comfort[1]; visit with the sick and administer to their relief, both spiritually and temporally[2]; visit with the discouraged, the fatherless, and the widows in their affliction[3]; support and encourage the weak; lift up the hands that hung down[4]; and strive to maintain a glad heart and a cheerful countenance[5] while doing so. All of these acts, which are not only the duties of a follower of Christ but also the fruits of a true understanding of the Atonement, are those that friends, family members, visiting teachers, and home teachers can do and should do.

Jesus said, "Look unto me in every thought; doubt not, fear not."[6] If His Atonement is the centerpiece of His mission, how do we do that?

---

1   See Mosiah 18:9.
2   See Mosiah 4:26.
3   See James 1:27.
4   See D&C 81:5.
5   See D&C 59:15.
6   D&C 6:36.

A SKETCH PAD AND AN ORPHANAGE—SERVICE AND THE ATONEMENT

This is my commandment,
That ye love one another, as I have loved you.

—John 15:12

Lori did not realize how closely she resembled her Savior one autumn night in Provo.

As Thanksgiving neared, our student ward visited a small nursing home to present a talent show to its residents. After arriving at the modest facility, we split up into groups and spread out through the home, visiting the residents in their rooms, inviting them to our performance, and, in some cases, helping them with their wheelchairs.

In the lobby, we rolled in a piano to create a makeshift performance area. We always had wonderfully talented people in our ward, and several shared their talents with the audience that night. Our master of ceremonies, Jimmy, kept the audience and performers laughing throughout the evening. I watched our small audience of residents and was pleased to see that they were enjoying the performances and the company of my students.

Only a few performances remained when Lori stood up to announce what she would do. She was a talented artist and had brought a large sketch pad. Lori said she would draw a caricature of one of the members of the audience. With a little coaxing, one of the women came to the front, and Lori helped her sit down in a chair.

Lori worked with quick pen strokes on her sketch pad. In a short time, she was finished and shyly displayed the sketch to the woman and then to the audience. It was a good likeness. The woman smiled, and her friends in the audience commented approvingly about the caricature. At the woman's request, Lori signed the drawing. Lori announced that she would draw sketches for anyone else who would like them after the talent show.

The last musical number ended, and we said a prayer. The students stayed to talk with the residents. After some initial awkwardness, the residents began to open up and seemed to enjoy the conversations.

I noticed that a large crowd had gathered around Lori. She was sitting on the floor with her sketch pad on her knees. Many residents wanted to have their portraits drawn and were happy to wait. Most were women. As each woman sat down for her portrait, Lori would speak with her. Sometimes the woman asked about Lori's studies and her future plans. As they conversed, Lori looked carefully into the face of each of her subjects, seeking to find unique features to highlight in her simple drawings.

The contrast between artist and subject was immense. Lori's bright young face was beautiful and radiant. Her body was strong and healthy. She could walk and run effortlessly and had many active years of life and a world of opportunities ahead of her. Some young men already wanted to marry her, and, after completing a mission, she undoubtedly would say yes to one of them.

The women Lori was drawing were old. None could run and many could not walk. Disease limited their activities, and most lived on modest means. In some cases their families ignored them. The faces Lori drew bore lines of worry, pain, and grief. For them, each day was very much like the previous one had been and like the next one would be. If young men had once asked them to marry, they were gone now. The women were carrying on as best they could under difficult circumstances, but most knew that their future on earth would be short and would not be very pleasant while it lasted.

Lori would look down at her sketch pad, make a few quick pen strokes, and then look back at each face with careful concentration. When Lori looked up, it seemed as if a kind, warm sun were briefly shining into each woman's life.

The other students finished speaking with the residents, put chairs away, and quietly left. Lori kept drawing. After Lori finished each sketch, the woman's friends would comment about how Lori had drawn her hair or the curve of the woman's chin just right, how she had captured the unique and individual features of their friend. Lori stayed long after the others had departed, until every woman who requested a portrait had received one.

Something wonderful had happened that night, and it wasn't about artistic talent. Not many people noticed the individuality of the residents of the nursing home. Some saw only one more old woman, a person of little consequence who would be forgotten a few moments later. The women were regarded as "patients," "residents," or "responsibilities" more than they were acknowledged as Jane or Mary or Emily.

Lori's vision was much different. She did not merely glance and then look away. She carefully observed each woman, noticing the many different features that made this person unique and different from any other daughter of God. She worked to capture that uniqueness on her sketch pad.

For an evening, Lori gave careful attention to women whom most others ignored. And the women basked in that attention. It was not so much the drawing that pleased them but rather the wonderful experience of being recognized for their distinctiveness. That recognition was the greatest gift Lori provided that night.

In a world of billions upon billions of people, we are each a unique son or daughter to our Heavenly Father. He knows us by name. When Jesus atoned for our sins, He did not do so for an undifferentiated accumulation of humanity. Somehow, a God with unnumbered children paid the price to save each of us, one by one.

Elder Merrill J. Bateman has said,

> For many years I thought of the Savior's experience in the garden and on the cross as places where a large mass of sin was heaped upon Him. Through the words of Alma, Abinadi, Isaiah, and other prophets, however, my view has changed. Instead of an impersonal mass of sin, there was a long line of people, as Jesus felt "our infirmities," (Heb. 4:15) "[bore] our griefs . . . carried our sorrows . . . [and] was bruised for our iniquities" (Isa. 53:4–5).

> The Atonement was an intimate, personal experience
> in which Jesus came to know how to help each of us.[1]

As we begin to understand—to really understand—the Atonement, as we come to comprehend that Christ has saved us from death and hell and the devil and endless torment,[2] as we grasp that without Him we are forever, irretrievably lost, a question begins to form in our mind. How can I repay Him? It is impossible, of course, for us ever to give our Savior anything but the tiniest, tiniest portion of what He has given us. But when we are grateful, deeply grateful, we want to demonstrate that gratitude in some way.

Three Commandments

Always remembering Him is a demonstration of our gratitude to the Lord. Taking upon ourselves His name and keeping His commandments is a demonstration of that gratitude. But what do those promises mean in daily life? What actions can we perform to show Him and ourselves that we are truly grateful and not just pretending to be grateful? The key to this answer lies in a commandment Christ gave three times.

After Jesus was crucified and resurrected, Peter and the other Apostles seemed confused at first, not knowing what they should do now that their precious leader was not with them daily. Perhaps Peter felt drawn back to his old ways before he was called by Christ, or perhaps he just needed to think, but he decided to go fishing.

Peter went to the Sea of Galilee, sometimes called the Sea of Tiberias, where he had fished many times before. He had been fishing on the Sea of Galilee when he first met Jesus. It was here that Jesus had called Peter and his brother Andrew to follow Him and become "fishers of men."[3]

On this much later occasion, Peter and other disciples boarded a boat and sailed out on the sea. They fished through the night but caught nothing.

"But when the morning was now come, Jesus stood on the shore: but the disciples knew not that it was Jesus. Then Jesus saith unto

---

1   Merrill J. Bateman, "A Pattern for All," *Ensign*, Nov. 2005, 75–76.

2   See 2 Ne. 9:26.

3   Matt. 4:19.

them, Children, have ye any meat? They answered him, No. And he said unto them, Cast the net on the right side of the ship, and ye shall find. They cast therefore, and now they were not able to draw it for the multitude of fishes. Therefore that disciple whom Jesus loved saith unto Peter, It is the Lord."[4]

Perhaps Peter remembered the earlier occasion when Jesus had told him where to cast his net, and it had been filled with fish.[5] Perhaps he remembered when he had walked on the water toward Jesus.[6] Powerful emotions had arisen in Peter's heart, and he wanted to be with his Savior. He immediately dived into the sea and swam toward Christ.

After the boat was brought to shore and the net emptied, the small group of fishermen gathered around a fire with the Savior, and He gave them bread and fish to eat. After they had finished eating, Jesus asked Peter a simple question, "Simon, son of Jonas, lovest thou me more than these?"

Peter answered, "Yea, Lord; thou knowest that I love thee." And Jesus replied, "Feed my lambs."

Jesus then asked another question. "He saith to him again the second time, Simon, son of Jonas, lovest thou me? He saith unto him, Yea, Lord; thou knowest that I love thee. He saith unto him, Feed my sheep.

"He saith unto him the third time, Simon, son of Jonas, lovest thou me? Peter was grieved because he said unto him the third time, Lovest thou me? And he said unto him, Lord, thou knowest all things; thou knowest that I love thee. Jesus saith unto him, Feed my sheep."[7]

Three almost identical questions. Three commandments: Feed my lambs, feed my sheep, feed my sheep.

When we have received a great blessing from God, when we have been forgiven of sin, when we have been saved from disaster, when our prayers for a loved one have been answered, when our appreciation for the many blessings we have received is overflowing, we express that gratitude to our Father in prayer. We feel an overwhelming

---

4   John 21:4–7.
5   See Luke 5:4–11.
6   See Matt. 14:25–31.
7   John 21:15–17.

love for our Father and our Savior, through whom these blessings have come. At that time we say with all our hearts, "I love thee, Lord." And if we listen carefully with our hearts, we will hear an echo from the shores of the Sea of Tiberias: "Feed my sheep."

VERTICAL AND HORIZONTAL

In order to appreciate how the Atonement works in our lives, it is helpful to divide it conceptually into two parts. The first is a vertical axis. We are at the bottom, and Christ is at the top. This demonstrates how the Atonement binds us to our Savior.

The Vertical Aspect of the Atonement

Christ

Me

If we think of the first principles of the gospel, we will understand this vertical relationship:

First, we must have faith in Christ, that through His Atonement He can save us if we look up to Him.

Second, because of our faith, we repent of our sins. We know that this is possible, that we can make such a great change because Christ has atoned for our sins and can remove their stains from us. Christ reaches down to forgive us and make it possible for us to move up, vertically, toward Him and our heavenly home.

Third, we are baptized to wash away the sins of which we have repented. Our baptism also acts as a witness that we have taken upon us the name of Christ because by doing so, Christ's Atonement reaches down to cleanse us. Christ recognizes that we have participated in this sacred ordinance, an ordinance that sets us apart from the rest of the world and allows us to be His followers. We renew our baptismal covenant each week as we take the sacrament. If we are repentant and humble, it is like being rebaptized, and we are cleansed and refreshed by the Atonement again.

Fourth, we receive the gift of the Holy Ghost. The Holy Ghost does many things in our lives, but His first and most important purpose is to testify of Christ, repeatedly turning our thoughts upward to the Savior and bringing words of inspiration and answers to prayers down that vertical axis to us.

The Atonement is the great unifying force between God and man, lifting us up, binding us to Christ, and helping us understand that He is the way, the upward way, the only way, past all of the pains of the world, past all of the temptations of Satan, back to our Father.

As Alma prophesied concerning the coming Christ, "And he shall go forth, suffering pains and afflictions and temptations of every kind; and this that the word might be fulfilled which saith *he will take upon him the pains and the sicknesses of his people.* And he will take upon him death, that he may loose the bands of death which bind his people; and *he will take upon him their infirmities,* that his bowels may be filled with mercy, according to the flesh, *that he may know according to the flesh how to succor his people according to their infirmities."*[8] Christ's Atonement elevates us on our best days and comforts and heals us on our worst days.

Once we understand and take into our hearts who Christ is and what He has done for us—when we have felt Him lift our sins, our pains, our sicknesses, and our infirmities and have felt Him give us renewed hope—we understand that Christ is the answer, the only true answer, to the sins, the sorrows, and the pains of every other person. This understanding changes us. We are consumed with a desire to help everyone understand the wonderful redemption and healing and peace of Christ that has changed our lives so miraculously. We realize that the commandment to feed His sheep includes a commandment for us to spread knowledge of His grace to those who need it. Whether they know it or not, every child of God desperately needs the grace of the Savior.

The sons of Mosiah experienced such a feeling after the miraculous conversion that saved them from their sins: "Now they were desirous that salvation should be declared to every creature,

---

8   Alma 7:11–12; emphasis added.

for they could not bear that any human soul should perish."⁹ This
desire took these faithful men on a long and difficult mission to the
Lamanites.

This desire to reach out to others is the horizontal axis of the
Atonement, traveling from person to person through testimony,
service, and love. Its purpose is to bring to others the wonderful
peace and love that we feel coming from our Savior. In the process of
so doing, both the person receiving service and the person providing
service feel the Savior's love.

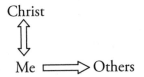

Christ linked the two aspects of the Atonement on several
occasions. He said, "A new commandment I give unto you, That ye
love one another; as I have loved you, that ye also love one another."¹⁰
In this scripture, Christ speaks of the vertical axis—"As I have loved
you"—and ties it directly to the horizontal axis—"love one another."

In His conversation with Peter on the shores of the Sea of
Tiberias, as found in John 21:15, Christ did the same thing: "Simon,
son of Jonas, lovest thou me? . . . Yea, Lord; thou knowest that I love
thee." Peter's love for his Savior runs up the vertical axis. When He
says, "Feed my sheep," Christ commands Peter to reach out along the
horizontal axis to take His love to the entire world.

If we need to feel the Atonement working in our lives, the most
reliable way to do so is to serve others. When I have counseled
someone who is in the process of repenting from a serious sin, I often
recommend that he or she make an effort to serve others. This isn't a
strategy for the repenting sinners to "earn their way" out of the sin.
Christ will forgive their sin not because they have earned forgiveness
but as an act of pure love, pure grace. However, by conscientiously
serving another, a repenting sinner can feel the Holy Ghost helping
him in that service, and the Holy Ghost carries Christ's approval and

---

9   Mosiah 28:3.
10   John 13:34.

love to the one who serves under such circumstances. For someone without any serious repentance to complete, the process works the same way—serve another, and feel the Atonement working in your life.

Satan tries to separate man from God. If we are alone without God and Christ, we are in the adversary's power. Satan tries to separate men from one another. In the Book of Mormon, we see how successful he was in separating the Lamanites from the Nephites. Satan's efforts continue in our day, separating nation from nation, race from race, class from class, men from women.

Christ's Atonement joins us—men to God and men to one another as brothers and sisters. As we become closer and closer to God along the vertical axis of the Atonement, both our yearning and our ability to bring the blessings of the Atonement to others grows along the horizontal axis. Our love for others increases as we comprehend the magnitude of the love that Heavenly Father and Christ have for us and as we come to understand that They have the same love for each of our brothers and sisters. We then desire to become the hands of God. We desire to constantly act as representatives of Christ wherever we are, be it through a smile, a kind word, or a helping hand.

God Is Here

Shannon was a wonderful returned missionary, majoring in music education and nearing graduation. One day she came into my bishop's office to talk about her plans. She had decided to travel to Romania to work in a hospital and orphanage for several months. We spoke about the work she would be doing and the reasons she felt this was where the Lord wanted her to serve. At her request, I gave her a blessing at the conclusion of our interview. During the blessing, I was strongly impressed by how much God loved Shannon and what a powerful representative of Christ she could be.

Shortly thereafter, Shannon left for Romania. I was privileged to receive e-mails from her describing her experiences as she adjusted to a new culture and unfamiliar work. She was growing and adapting, but service was sometimes difficult. Following is a portion of one of her e-mails, shared with her permission:

I think I've mentioned that we work in the mornings at an orphanage for handicapped children, and in the afternoon at the children's hospital with the abandoned babies as well as some of the older orphans.

Two weeks ago I was introduced there to a little boy named Alex. He was hooked up to four different machines and was obviously very, very sick. He was two years old. I spent a lot of time with him for the first three or four days and had some special experiences with him. Despite how unresponsive he usually seemed to be, he would gently squeeze my finger, and on my second day with him, he gave me the most adorable smile where I saw his perfect little baby teeth. In the middle of last week, his mom showed up at the hospital to take care of him, so I obviously deferred to her as the primary caregiver. But she loved for me to come in and spend time with him, as well, so I continued to go in and see him every day. His condition seemed to fluctuate a great deal. His heart rate was constantly changing, and the patterns of his breathing and heartbeat were different every day. I knew that he was very close to dying but was still unsure of his exact condition.

Today, right as I walked onto the third floor, his mother came running toward me, crying, telling me her son had died. My emotions have been so on edge lately that tears immediately filled my eyes. I don't know exactly when it happened, but I don't think it had been very long. She told me that the funeral would be tomorrow, and she would leave the hospital tomorrow morning. When I asked if she had any family here, she told me they had left. My heart went out to this woman, and I felt empathy in a whole new way.

She wanted me to go see Alex, and after that I needed to step outside for a while.

Once my emotions were under control I just sat there and felt the wind on my face and listened to the rustling leaves. One of the biggest things that I've been struggling with lately is just how hard life is here in Romania, and, specifically, how much pain and suffering goes on at this hospital. I suppose I was feeling bitterness and resentment toward this country for allowing the problem to get this bad. But as these feelings were again going through my head combined with the emotions of Alex dying, my spirit at once became very still. I was suddenly aware of God's power through this incredible wind that had kicked up. It was quite strong and made a very loud rustling through the trees, and I felt the realization. *God is here, too, and He loves these people.* So much *more* than I know. His power is here, and one day He will heal all of the suffering and pain. It helped me feel that I did not have to take on so much grief and pain because He already had.

As the Spirit reinforced this knowledge over and over, the wind grew stronger and stronger, and a few times became incredibly powerful. It was as if God Himself was bearing witness to me that He has not forgotten these people. *He is here.*

I sat there for quite a while, letting this manifestation sink in. But I soon began feeling that I needed to walk back inside those hospital doors and be with the other children who are still in so much need. I didn't know if I would be able to. I was worried that my emotions would take over and I would upset the boys even more. But then the thought came to me that *one of the ways that God is here is because I am here.* That is, He needs me in those hospital rooms sharing His love and peace. It all came together in a way I can't describe, and I felt the whole experience make sense in a meaningful way that would be futile to try to explain.

By this time the wind had dried my tears, and I knew I could go back inside. Mihai made a lot of progress in writing his name today. I taught Florin how to thumb wrestle and he loved it, and George was just his normal goofy self. Although I do feel somewhat drained, I am at peace.

What profound spiritual rewards await us as we serve others: "One of the ways that God is here is because I am here." We are the hands of God when we share the gospel with those who have not received it. We are the hands of God when we reach out to "succor the weak, lift up the hands which hang down, and strengthen the feeble knees."[11] We can be instruments through which His love is manifested to those who most need to feel it. We can have the privilege of playing a role in bringing the healing and strengthening blessings of the Atonement into the lives of those whose hearts and lives can be rescued only by their Savior.

"And thus they were instruments in the hands of God in bringing many to the knowledge of the truth, yea, to the knowledge of their Redeemer. And how blessed are they! For they did publish peace; they did publish good tidings of good; and they did declare unto the people that the Lord reigneth."[12]

PURE RELIGION

Whenever one of the members of my ward was having problems—academic challenges; dating/non-dating struggles; or repentance issues—as I mentioned earlier, I almost always suggested that a part of the solution lay in serving others. In our ward, our most important auxiliary committee was dedicated to service. We called it the "Pure Religion Committee," based upon James 1:27: "Pure religion and undefiled before God and the Father is this, To visit the fatherless and widows in their affliction, and to keep himself unspotted from the world."

The service provided was important to those who received it, but I had another reason for encouraging service. The troubled men and women in my ward needed to feel the influence of the Atonement in their lives. One of the most reliable ways of bringing the Atonement into their lives was for them to provide service to others. When they served others, the Holy Ghost almost always came to them during and after that service. President Henry B. Eyring has said, "When [the Holy Ghost] is your companion, you can have confidence that the Atonement is working in your life."[13]

---

11   D&C 81:5.

12   Mosiah 27:36–37.

13   "Come unto Christ," fireside address given at Brigham Young University on 29 Oct. 1989.

Whether we are students or not, it is so easy for our lives to become unbalanced and for the Spirit's quiet voice to be drowned out by other, louder noises. Focusing on the needs of another person, someone who needs our assistance, helps quiet the outside noises and allows the Holy Ghost, through the Atonement, to heal our souls. President Marion G. Romney said, "Receiving the Holy Ghost is the therapy which effects forgiveness and heals the sin-sick soul."[14] It also heals the weary and discouraged soul. I have seen faces shine with the light of our Savior's love as my ward members served others.

Some of the poorest members of our community are Hispanic immigrants who have difficulty understanding the language, customs, and institutions of a new land. When Christ was on the earth, He always served the poor. Striving to be humble followers of Jesus Christ, our ward members also tried to serve the poor.

At the beginning of my last year as bishop, we searched for a better way to serve the poor who were Latinos. After much discussion and prayer, the Lord led us to the president of a Spanish-speaking branch. On the day we first visited him, President Carter was praying for specific help for the youth in his branch. He told us, "Some of the youth in my ward don't understand how important it is for them to work hard in school, and they are getting terrible grades. Many of their parents are not able to provide the help their children need because the parents never had the opportunity to get a good education."

President Carter spoke of a young man in his branch who was likely to drop out of high school. When the president tried to convince him of how important his education was, the young man responded, "I'm only a Mexican. When I grow up, I'm going to be a laborer like my parents. I don't need school for that."

President Carter told me, "Many of the fathers in our branch work two jobs that require sixty to eighty hours a week. Many mothers also work long hours outside of the home. Their schedules make it hard for them to spend time with their families and almost impossible for them to hold a Church calling. I want something different for their children. I don't want their children to be laborers in the factories; I want their children to *own* the factories. They need education for that."

---

14   "The Holy Ghost," *Ensign*, May 1974, 92.

Our ward quickly prepared plans to provide tutoring and homework help for the children and teenagers of the branch. President Carter promoted the tutoring program in his branch, and I did the same in our ward, asking members to come and teach. Some of my students worried that they were not trained teachers. I responded that if they had grades good enough to be admitted to BYU, they knew everything necessary to help an elementary or high school student with homework.

We scheduled the first session on a Wednesday evening at 7:00 PM in the Primary rooms of the branch's building. We arrived early, said a prayer, and set up tables and chairs in the empty rooms.

At seven a few children arrived, looking dubious, as did their parents. One of our members greeted them in their choice of Spanish or English and asked what help the children needed with their schoolwork. Soon more children arrived. The time passed quickly as I walked from room to room to monitor how things were going. Because of their willingness to serve, my students' natural abilities were magnified as the Spirit joined them in their work, making connections and helping each child feel welcome and comfortable. President Carter was also observing, and we shared our thoughts throughout the evening.

After the children left, we held a meeting with the tutors to talk about what had worked and what hadn't. The tutors spoke about some of the children. One tutor remarked, "I was helping a little boy who receives nothing but Ds and Fs. He's really smart, but he just doesn't understand the importance of doing his homework." The Spirit was strong. I felt it and knew that its influence was impacting my ward members.

We realized that rather than working with small groups of children, the best way to help was to have one tutor for each child. That idea felt good to me. The Savior taught large groups of people, but some of His most inspiring work was performed one-on-one, speaking with a single person. President Carter said he would urge more of his branch members to bring their children, and I said I would recruit more tutors for the next week.

During our second week, the evening went more smoothly. Many of my students were already starting to magnify their callings, coming up with their own tutoring ideas, and doing more than I asked them to do. Some brought teaching materials they had purchased themselves. One put up signs on the doors of each room—math, English, science—to show the children where to go for help in specific subjects. More of the children brought their homework assignments.

During our evaluation, we realized that elementary school homework often required a computer connected to the Internet, something we had not anticipated. Many of the families in the branch couldn't afford computers. The school teachers suggested that the children use the computers at the city library, but when parents worked evening jobs and older children were needed to babysit younger children, this wasn't possible. Every missed computer research assignment was another F.

After a little inspired persuasion and an explanation that computer use would be constantly supervised, the stake president allowed us to tap into the Family History Library's Internet connection during the time we were tutoring. Several of my students brought their laptops, and we set up a computer lab in the high council room for students and for their parents.

We helped students with their assignments and showed parents how they could look up their children's assignments and grades on the school district's website. When parents saw how low some of the grades were, they discussed missing assignments with their children. We explained to the parents that teachers would often permit students to make up missed assignments so grades could quickly improve. Some of my Spanish-speaking ward members offered to attend parent-teacher conferences with parents to make certain that they clearly understood what the teachers were suggesting about how their children could improve.

The tutoring program continued to become more popular. One of our native Spanish speakers waited by the front door so she could greet families who were coming for the first time and reassure nervous parents. We brought more and more materials for our tutoring, including books, pencils, and flash cards. We organized activities for preschool children so parents could bring all their children and so older children who had babysitting duties could still receive tutoring.

We learned that some of the children wanted help with music lessons, and we had lots of musicians in our ward. One Primary room echoed with the sounds of simultaneous clarinet, flute, and violin practice sessions. On many evenings, we used every piano in the building for piano lessons.

Children who were not members of the branch began to attend after the city library and some of the schools spread the word about our program. At President Carter's request one Sunday, we sent a large group of returned missionaries and prospective missionaries from our ward to distribute fliers describing the tutoring program to all the Spanish-speaking homes within the branch boundaries.

One of the most gratifying aspects of our service occurred as I watched bonds of love grow between my ward members and the children they taught. Children sought out their particular tutor each week. One evening I watched as one of the students in my ward sat with the child he taught regularly and took turns reading verses from the Book of Mormon.

Most of the tutors weren't having any particular problems in their personal lives, but I knew that a few were struggling with discouragement and other problems. As they served, I could see the Atonement lifting and strengthening them. When the Holy Ghost came to help these men and women teach a child, He also soothed and healed the soul of the teacher.

It never felt like a sacrifice for me to spend an evening at President Carter's branch. In fact, I looked forward to Wednesday nights. Of course, I enjoyed seeing the Latino children and teenagers, but my greatest pleasure came from watching my ward members as they served. They were so spiritually graceful, so kind, and so skillful in their service, and the children just loved being around them. With a bishop's eye, I could see the Lord lifting my members to a higher plane, a better place, while they served. At times, I seemed to glimpse who they would be in the future, in a world more exalted than this one, surrounded by spirit children of their own.

The Atonement can be extraordinarily powerful when we help others. Even though Mother Teresa was never a Latter-day Saint during her lifetime, her service brought the influence of the Atonement into her life and raised her to a level of spirituality that even a secular world recognized.

Almost everyone goes through periods in their life when it seems as if the Spirit has become more distant. Spiritual experiences may have been powerful in the past, but now they seem weak or even nonexistent. Prayer becomes difficult and may seem mechanical. We wonder if our prayers will ever be answered. There are many things we should do when we find ourselves in such a condition—scripture study, church attendance, and more focused prayer immediately come to mind. However, one of the most powerful ways I have witnessed for people to pull themselves out of a spiritual slump is to serve others. The Holy Ghost will come as we serve. As President Eyring has informed us, when we feel the Holy Ghost, we can be confident that the Atonement is working in our lives, healing us, cleansing us, lifting us, helping us to see by a brighter light and know that our Savior loves us.[15]

As fall semester drew to a close, we received an invitation from President Carter. "We would like to invite your ward to our Christmas social to show our appreciation for the help you have given us. We'll provide the food. You won't believe how wonderful it tastes." When I asked what our ward could contribute to the social, he said my students could help with the entertainment.

President Carter was right about the food. Each of the women in the branch brought her best recipe, and the food tasted better than anything I have eaten at any other Church social.

When the time for entertainment arrived, we were happy to watch young women from the branch whom we had come to know from our tutoring perform a medley of dances from various Latin countries. After they were finished, members of our ward demonstrated their many and varied talents in music, juggling, and dancing like a robot, which the young children loved.

We concluded by performing the Christmas story in costume as a Primary might present it. Sophisticated and intelligent college students were happy to dress as Mary, Joseph, the Wise Men, shepherds, donkeys, sheep, cattle, and even a mouse. I read the Christmas story in English as one of my ward members translated it into Spanish. The Spirit was strong because a bond of love had grown through service. Both those who provided service and those who were served felt the love of the Lord.

Many of the members of this Spanish branch were poor. Someone who was seeking ways to help those people could easily have concluded

15   See Henry B. Erying, "Come unto Christ," fireside address.

that assisting them required money. My student ward didn't have any money. Most of my members were working their way through college and lived on tight budgets themselves. While we didn't have much money, we did have knowledge, talent, and energy. And we loved the Lord. His Atonement magnified that love a thousandfold, and He poured it back into each of us. Though several years have passed, I can still feel the love the Savior gave me while serving that branch.

How We Serve

In my home stake and community, I am privileged to live with people who provide wonderful service in distant countries. With great effort and love, these people provide dental treatments in Guatemala, build orphanages in Haiti, and add bathrooms to Mexican homes that have none.

A brother who helped organize the building of an orphanage in Haiti inspired our student ward members with his experiences and with his dedication in serving the children there. Several of my students traveled to Mexico to improve the homes of the very poor in that country and presented wonderful firesides about their experiences.

For twenty-five years, my wife, G.G., had suffered from serious, at times disabling, clinical depression. As she deepened her understanding of the Atonement and heard of this wonderful service provided in distant lands, she felt a strong urge to participate. She wanted to work in the hot sun and dirt of the Mexican desert to help those in need, and she desired to feel the Spirit that came with such work.

But her illness would not permit her to provide such service. Traveling and living in a poor part of the world was dangerous for her health, and the chance of a severe depressive episode far away from appropriate treatment was too great for her to leave the United States. G.G. felt discouraged because she could not help those who had less than she did, and more particularly because she knew the importance of service to others in magnifying the effects of the Atonement in her life.

During my last year on campus, G.G. experienced a miraculous healing from her long illness. A bright dawn came into her life after a long, dark, terrible night. Her strength returned. Her mind was active and free.

Now she could serve others without disability. But how should she serve? Was this the time to travel to Mexico? G.G. began to write about her experiences—about her depression, about her recovery, and about the central role that the Atonement played in her life. She is a gifted writer, and many of her essays were published in *Meridian Magazine,* an online publication for LDS readers.

Many people wrote to G.G., responding to her articles. G.G. was able to help them understand what they were experiencing with their own depression or how they could assist others as they supported loved ones who suffered from this terrible disease. Her readers communicated their gratitude to her for writing about this difficult subject. Together with our son, Greg, and myself, G.G. wrote a book, *Deliverance from Depression: Finding Hope and Healing Through the Atonement of Christ,* in which each of us spoke about how essential the Atonement was in enduring and overcoming this difficult disease and how much our Savior helped us during that long and trying time.

As G.G. prayed and pondered, she came to understand that her most important service, her personal mission for this time in her life, was not in Mexico or Haiti. The place she was to labor was at her keyboard. She did not need to board a plane to serve others. The Lord wanted her to walk to her home office, pray, sit down, and serve His children from that location.

Caring for a dying child in Romania, visiting elderly women in a nursing home, teaching Latino children who need help with homework, donating dental work in Guatemala, building an orphanage in Haiti, putting up new bathrooms in Mexico, typing on a computer in Provo—opportunities to serve are everywhere. There will never be a shortage of people needing help. All of this service is encompassed in Christ's commandment to Peter and to us to feed His sheep.

Our Savior wants us to learn something of what He knows by having us help Him do His work. Paul urges us to have "the mind of Christ."[16] Christ saved the world and everyone in it. He asks us to help save God's sons and daughters one at a time from loneliness,

---

16 1 Cor. 2:16.

suffering, ignorance, and the many other afflictions that accompany life in a mortal world. In that process and under His divine influence, our hearts are changed, and we become a little more like our Savior. Through our service, we take His name upon us and feel His love for those in need flow through us to them. We cannot be a conduit for His love without being profoundly blessed by that experience. And as we communicate His love to others, we understand more clearly how much He loves us.

> *Inasmuch as ye have done it unto one of the*
> *least of these my brethren, ye have done it unto me.*

—Matthew 25:40

ALL THINGS TESTIFY OF CHRIST—SCRIPTURE STUDY AND THE ATONEMENT

*[Jesus Christ's] Atonement is the
greatest event in human history. There is nothing to
compare with it. It is the most fundamental part of our Father's
plan for the happiness of His children.*

—President Gordon B. Hinckley, "Inspirational Thoughts," *Ensign,* Sept. 2007, 8

*The Atonement of the Lord Jesus Christ is the heart
and core and center of revealed religion.*

—Elder Bruce R. McConkie, "Christ and the Creation," *Ensign,* June 1982, 9

*For the natural man is an enemy to God,
and has been from the fall of Adam, and will be, forever
and ever, unless he yields to the enticings of the Holy Spirit, and
putteth off the natural man and becometh a saint through
the atonement of Christ the Lord.*

—Mosiah 3:19

I learned a lot about becoming better at changing from the members of my BYU singles ward. In a week, my members could change majors, boyfriends, girlfriends, roommates, apartments, graduate schools, and future job plans. And when the Spirit called them to change their lives and turn back to their Heavenly Father and Savior with complete commitment, they could rapidly accomplish that change, as well.

We are accustomed to thinking about the permanent and unchanging aspects of the gospel, and there are many enduring principles that applied to Adam and Eve just as they apply to us. However, in the midst of this eternal doctrine, we can sometimes forget that the gospel of Jesus Christ is the greatest force for change in the universe.

Since we reside in mortal bodies in a fallen world, we're pre-programmed to be natural men and women. Our most important job in this life is to *change*—to put off the natural man or woman and become Saints—and the only way we can do that is through the power of the Atonement of Christ.

Much like my students, we need to become adept at exchanging bad for good and good for better. Sometimes that requires letting go of bad attitudes, bad habits, and large or small sins that we have become accustomed to incorporating in our lives. There can be something dangerous about becoming too comfortable with such flaws. *I wasn't struck down by lightning yesterday because of my little problem,* we think, *so I'll probably be fine today, as well.*

Alma understood the changes necessary to deal with our familiar frailties. "Yea, I say unto you come and fear not, and *lay aside every sin, which easily doth beset you,* which doth bind you down to destruction, yea, come and go forth, and show unto your God that *ye are willing to repent of your sins and enter into a covenant with him to keep his commandments,* and witness it unto him this day by going into the waters of baptism."[1]

Each of us experiences a constant downward pull as we live inside mortal bodies on a mortal planet. Sometimes that pull is stronger, and sometimes it is weaker, but in some way it is always present. That downward pull will turn even the best of us into natural men and natural women unless we constantly strive to offset it with an upward spiritual movement toward the Savior. If we listen, the Holy Ghost will remind us of what we should be doing and will help us move upward, but the initial effort must be ours.

Putting off the natural man is not something we do once or twice in our lives; it requires a daily, sometimes hourly, sometimes minute-by-minute effort. We can't become saints in a single giant leap and

---

1   Alma 7:15; emphasis added.

then sit back and relax. We must constantly be working at that saintly becoming, sometimes moving forward, at other times working our way back from a downward slide. Becoming, changing, moving to be a better person is the core activity of our mortal lives, and we cannot make those vital and constant changes without the strength the Atonement provides.

Another term describing the Atonement, *grace,* is defined in the Bible Dictionary, in part, as follows:

> Grace. A word that occurs frequently in the New Testament, especially in the writings of Paul. The main idea of the word is *divine means of help or strength,* given through the bounteous mercy and love of Jesus Christ.
>
> It is through the grace of the Lord Jesus, made possible by his atoning sacrifice, that mankind will be raised in immortality, every person receiving his body from the grave in a condition of everlasting life. It is likewise through the grace of the Lord that individuals, *through faith in the atonement of Jesus Christ* and repentance of their sins, *receive strength and assistance to do good works that they otherwise would not be able to maintain if left to their own means. This grace is an enabling power* that allows men and women to lay hold on eternal life and exaltation after they have expended their own best efforts.[2]

Speaking of this definition, Elder David A. Bednar said, "Thus, *the enabling and strengthening aspect of the Atonement* helps us to see and to do and to become good in ways that we could never recognize or accomplish with our limited mortal capacity."[3]

The Atonement, this divine power that allows and empowers us to do what would otherwise be impossible, gives us the ability to change from what we are to what we know we should be and to overcome our lost and fallen state, our estrangement from all that is eternally most dear to us. Part of that change involves using the scriptures in

---

2   Bible Dictionary, s.v. "Grace"; emphasis added.
3   "In the Strength of the Lord," *Ensign,* Nov. 2004, 77; emphasis added.

different ways, more redemptive ways, and watching for ways they can connect us to this great strengthening power.

Be Still and Know That I Am God

As I was undergoing a serious personal trial, I worried about it constantly. This problem monopolized my thoughts, often making it difficult to sleep. It was easy for me to imagine catastrophic consequences if I failed to find a solution. I vividly visualized ruin in my future.

I prayed often and hard for answers in the morning, at night, and throughout the day. I rolled the problem over and over in my mind. I traveled a well-worn path through my troubles, seeing the horror of them, feeling my doubt, asking for help, thinking about the same possible, yet impossible, solutions. After I finished one circuit of my worries, I began another. If ever a problem was studied out in my mind, this one was. But I could see no resolution.

Weeks passed. The problem grew worse, and no answers came. In addition to heartfelt prayers, I read the scriptures daily, according to my normal practice, but no answers came from that source. Mentally, I was in a downward spiral that seemed to have no end.

Then one morning, I woke with a scripture in my mind, "All flesh is in mine hands." I was only vaguely familiar with that scripture and did not know where it was located. I immediately got up, searched, and found Doctrine and Covenants 101:16, "Therefore, let your hearts be comforted concerning Zion; for all flesh is in mine hands; be still and know that I am God."

Instead of retracing my problems over and over in my mind, I started repeating the scripture, particularly the last part, over and over. *"All flesh is in mine hands; be still and know that I am God."* When my anxiety began to rise, I would bring those words to my mind. *"All flesh is in mine hands; be still and know that I am God."*

This was a message for me, delivered in my sleep because that was the only time the Spirit could push through my ceaseless worrying. I will never know how many times the Lord had tried to deliver that message earlier but was blocked by a mind completely occupied with other things—"important" things, natural-man things. I had been praying, but I hadn't been carefully listening for answers.

A feeling of calm, absent for many weeks, began to come over me. I *was* in the Lord's hands. He had died to redeem my body from mortal death and to give me an opportunity, conditioned on my obedience, to have a much different celestial body in the future. But this promise was not just about the future. A Savior who can resurrect a body from the dead can also strengthen and enlighten and guide that mortal body away from any kind of danger or trial. He was not announcing the end of my trial, but He was giving me strength for the trial.

He is the Son of God, a God of miracles, a God who rules the universe, including my tiny little portion. *His* job was to be my Lord and Savior, and He was very good at His job. He had already atoned for all my fears and their accompanying pain. *My* job was to be still, quiet, and calm and to focus my obsessive thinking on remembering, in my mind and in my heart, that He was God so He could give me strength. *My* job was to listen very carefully.

The Lord seems to deliver some of His most important messages a still and quiet voice. When He was releasing Nephi and Lehi from imprisonment and calling the Lamanites to repentance, the Savior's voice "was not a voice of thunder, neither was it a voice of a great tumultuous noise, but behold, it was a still voice of perfect mildness, as if it had been a whisper."[4] In a world filled with a cacophony of contending messages, each message louder than the last, a world in which very few people seem to want to listen, we must step away from carnal habits to sit very still and just hear. And in that hearing, we must give up all ideas of "my will" or "my way" to receive the words of life that Christ has for us if we just listen.

My difficult problem was not solved immediately. I held on to my message, my personal scripture, and burned it into my mind, but the problem was not at an end. Over time, part of me remained calm, but a growing part of me began to worry again. I began to become more noisy inside as the natural man in me was working to throw off the restraints the spiritual man was trying to keep in place.

Was my message, my revelation in scripture, not really a signal that the end of my trial would come quickly? Was it a small drink of water in a desert that stretched for miles and miles before me? I

---

4 Helaman 5:30.

doubted. I did not doubt the significance or origin of my early morning revelation—those were clear—but without fully realizing it, I was beginning to doubt my security in the hands of the Lord. It is incredibly foolish when expressed in those terms, and I could not have stated it that way at the time, but that feeling had crept into my thoughts.

The Lord told the Apostle Thomas, the one who doubted, "Be not faithless."[5] I was not completely faithless, but I was a little more faithless than I had been a few days earlier. I thought about Job and wondered if the Lord had a rough road for me to travel.

Then on a new morning, another scripture was in my mind as I awoke. "Look unto me in every thought; doubt not, fear not." The experience was just as before. I knew this scripture but had forgotten about it. There it was in Doctrine and Covenants 6:36, "Look unto me in every thought; doubt not, fear not." Then I read on to verse 37, *"Behold the wounds which pierced my side, and also the prints of the nails in my hands and feet; be faithful, keep my commandments, and ye shall inherit the kingdom of heaven"* (emphasis added).

There it was. The Atonement. The Spirit was reminding me how great a sacrifice the Savior made to save me. *Behold,* the Spirit said, *pay attention to what Christ has done for you. He carries the scars of the wounds in His side, His hands, and His feet, the wounds He suffered for everyone in the world, including you.*

As I read those two verses over and over, I understood why they were together, the reason that I didn't need to doubt or fear. I had a Savior. He had suffered and died for me and taken upon Himself all of my pains and fears. Whatever trials I had faced or would ever face, Christ had already experienced. I could look unto Him without doubt or fear because of what He had done for me. Whatever future difficulties I was going to experience, my Lord would help me through those difficulties because He had already been there. They might be hard, but if I looked to my Savior, they would never be too hard for me to bear; my Savior would be with me through those trials, and He had suffered much, much worse. My trials would never destroy me if I would just look to Jesus. Just look and remember the prints of the nails. Those prints were for me.

---

5   John 20:27.

In the midst of my trials, Satan wanted me to look at my surroundings and circumstances and feel fear. Christ wanted me to look to Him and fear not.

This new scripture became a familiar part of my daily prayers and thoughts. Along with my previous revelatory scripture, I repeated the messages I had received over and over, and they sank down deep, really deep, in my heart.

The internal peace and calm that I felt finally allowed the Spirit to reach me while I was awake. A few days after my second scripture, I was prompted to take a very unusual step, one I normally never would have considered. I took that step, and then another. I was moving into unfamiliar territory. I needed guidance, and it came. I could not see the end of the path I was on. Often I had to wait to even see the next step. Since I didn't understand the path, I acknowledged that I required constant direction. I kept remembering that my job was to be still, to listen, not to doubt, not to fear and that the Savior's job was all the other things. After a few more steps into areas that were unlighted and appeared unpromising to me but were known to the Lord, my difficult trial was over.

THE STORY ALWAYS CONTINUES

Quite often, a written or spoken story of the miraculous Atonement, of our Lord acting in our lives, would end at this point, but that could give the wrong impression. The incorrect impression would be that I lived happily ever after, that I no longer desperately needed the grace of my Savior every moment of every day, that I could read my scriptures on Sunday and be adequately strengthened and guided. I hope that I have moved to a higher level of understanding and obedience because of this wonderful experience, but I cannot ever take that for granted. I need a Savior, and you need a Savior. Always. Every breath of every day.

My special revelation, my miraculous solution, was not the end of all trials. I had not found a magic key that eliminated challenges from my life. In this mortal life, trials ebb and flow, but they do not end entirely. However, through a better understanding of the Atonement, we gain strength to better deal with the trials we encounter.

In the Church, we are accustomed to relying upon things that do not change—the nature and character of God, the reality of Jesus Christ, the principles of salvation. However, if we extend the unchanging character of these truths to ourselves, if we believe that once we have found one important answer we enter into a secure and comfortable spiritual holding pattern, we make a great error. In mortal life, we never retire to a spiritual house on the beach.

As a natural man or natural woman, we need to change and change a lot, likely throughout all of our earthly lives. We are dual beings—spirits, whose spiritual parents are pure and perfect, living within mortal bodies built from the impure elements of this world. This duality pulls us in different directions. Our spirits, if we keep them strong enough, strive to pull us upward toward our Heavenly Parents. Our bodies, our precious bodies for which we waited so long, provide an ongoing test by exerting a downward pull because of their earthly components, challenging our spirits to exercise ongoing control and direction. The Holy Ghost acts upon our spirits if we allow Him to do so, while Satan tempts us through our bodies and the carnal aspects of earthly life.

Unless we are always striving to move upward and actively accessing the enabling power of the Atonement to do so, we inevitably slide downward, sometimes slowly and sometimes with breathtaking rapidity. However much we are a friend of God today, we will begin to become an enemy tomorrow unless we draw a little closer, serve a little better, understand a little more today through the Atonement. Part of this perpetual changing requires that we allow the scriptures to lift us upward.

How can the Atonement affect our approach to studying the scriptures daily? If we understand our present condition and why we need the Atonement, we will approach the scriptures as a traveler would a guidebook for returning home. We need to find and follow reliable guides—our Heavenly Father, our Savior Jesus Christ, and Their messenger, the Holy Ghost. If we are ever to make it home, threading our way through the trials and temptations of this life, we need direction at every step. Because of ongoing bumps and obstacles on our journey, we may find ourselves on a different spiritual plane almost every time we open the scriptures. Between our last serious study of the scriptures and today, we may have taken some steps in a strange direction and may require divine instruction on how to get back to safety.

We cannot search the scriptures only a single time and understand which path we must take. We will encounter many, many turnings on our road back to our heavenly home and must carefully study our scriptural guidebook and listen to the Spirit that such study invites so we do not miss a critical turn.

We do not know in advance when we will encounter a fork in our mortal road. We may not even immediately recognize that we have arrived at a fork, at an important life choice. We must read the scriptures daily so we are prepared to take the proper path when the time for decision comes suddenly. If we have traveled down the wrong road, we must look carefully in our guidebook to find the way back so we can again continue along the right road.

There are so many unfamiliar places in our travels. As we search for clues to the *terra incognita,* the unknown territories of our life's journey, we always look for the Savior, knowing that our way home will always lead to Jesus, and He, in turn, will always lead us forward. If we hold on to the Savior, He will carry us home. His Atonement allows Him to promise, "I am the way, the truth, and the life: no man cometh unto the Father, but by me."[6]

As we read the scriptures, we put off our natural selves and strive in our study to be "submissive, meek, humble, patient, full of love, willing to submit to all things which the Lord seeth fit to inflict upon [us]."[7] We quell pride, doubt, and impatience and act as though we are sitting at the Savior's feet while He reads the words of the scriptures to us.

ALL THINGS TESTIFY OF CHRIST

Remembering that the scripture's main purpose is to testify of Christ and His Atonement, we always watch for those testimonies. If we do so, we will find them everywhere. The lost who are found, the prisoners who are freed, and the condemned who are saved testify

6   John 14:6.
7   Mosiah 3:19.

of the Atonement. Redemption, salvation, grace, rescue, repentance, mercy, forgiveness, sacrifice, love, exodus, and return all testify of Christ's Atonement.

Atonement scriptures provide a powerful, redemptive spiritual and emotional bond between ourselves and our Savior. We are the lost sheep who are found. We are Lazarus to be called forth from the grave. We are the sinners who find forgiveness at the feet of Jesus. We are the lepers who are cleansed.

In many instances, we find testimonies of the Atonement directly expressed by ancient prophets. Job testifies, "For I know that my redeemer liveth, and that he shall stand at the latter day upon the earth: And though after my skin worms destroy this body, yet in my flesh shall I see God: Whom I shall see for myself, and mine eyes shall behold."[8]

Alma speaks passionately about the Only Being who can save us. "And it came to pass that as I was thus racked with torment, while I was harrowed up by the memory of my many sins, behold, I remembered also to have heard my father prophesy unto the people concerning the coming of one *Jesus Christ, a Son of God, to atone for the sins of the world.* Now, as my mind caught hold upon this thought, *I cried within my heart: O Jesus, thou Son of God, have mercy on me,* who am in the gall of bitterness, and am encircled about by the everlasting chains of death. And now, behold, *when I thought this, I could remember my pains no more;* yea, I was harrowed up by the memory of my sins no more."[9]

In addition to the testimonies directly expressed throughout the scriptures, we also find testimonies of the Atonement that are symbolically expressed. In the Old Testament, each of the many sacrifices described points to the Atoning sacrifice that would come. For example, the redemption of the children of Israel from bondage in Egypt is a parable of the Atonement. In the New Testament, in addition to the words and actions of Christ, we can see the tremendous power the Lord gives to His faithful servant Paul and how Paul draws on that power to preach and testify despite tremendous physical trials. That power is available through the Atonement.

The Book of Mormon is another testament of Jesus Christ in large part because it is a testament of the Atonement. Nowhere else in ancient

---

8   Job 19:25–27.

9   Alma 36:17–19; emphasis added.

scripture do we find such rich detail or powerful teachings about the Atonement as we do in the words of Jacob, King Benjamin, Abinadi, and Alma. Additionally, we have the words and example of the resurrected Christ to teach us of His sacrifice. In the Doctrine and Covenants, we see how the enabling power of the Atonement transforms an uneducated farm boy into the first Prophet of the last dispensation. We also witness how well the Lord knows His servants and how much He cares for them. The Pearl of Great Price shows us that before the earth was even created, the Savior was chosen to perform the Atonement and that the Atonement would be the central event of the earth's existence.

Once we come to an appreciation of the Atonement, we see this doctrine taught everywhere. While we should study many different aspects of the scriptures, there is nothing more important to learn from them than the central fact that Christ loved us enough to suffer and die in order to save us from sin and death and to open the path back to our Heavenly Father.

LETTERS FROM HOME

In order to successfully follow the path back to Heavenly Father, we need a constant stream of messages and reminders from Him and our Savior. If we look unto the Savior in every thought, those messages will continue, for He is anxious to help us. But if our attention wanders—and we all have to fight against spiritual attention deficit—the messages will be less frequent and more difficult to understand.

If our earth life is like being away at school for a season, then the scriptures can be likened to an enormous collection of letters from our heavenly home.[10] We are able to open and understand those letters only by regularly reading them with the assistance of the Holy Ghost, who is an instrument of the enabling power of the Atonement. Without the Holy Ghost and without consistent, ongoing effort on our part, the scriptures remain a stack of sealed envelopes. We may understand that they are letters from home, but their contents will be unavailable to us.

---

10   See Bruce C. Hafen, "The Atonement: All for All," *Ensign,* May 2004, 97–99; see also Ardeth G. Kapp, "The Holy Scriptures: Letters from Home," *Ensign,* Nov. 1985, 93–94.

If we look to Jesus in every thought, we will be anxious to read and reread the scriptures, to open a letter each day, knowing that the same verses we read last month can carry a new message for us today. Our Heavenly Father knows us, and He knows how to send us exactly the right letter at precisely the right time.

The Savior tells us, "The words that I speak unto you, they are spirit, and they are life."[11] There is never a time, never a moment, when we do not need the divine words of life found in the scriptures. They are the words of life because they testify of Christ and His Atonement, our only path to eternal life.

Sometimes we feel far removed from our heavenly origins; the separation seems so great. At those times, we need to hear our Savior's voice and know His words. Every day, more than anything else, we need to continue to hear His voice through the scriptures.

If we hear His voice, then we can know, regardless of whatever dark chasms surround us, that we will not perish because He knows the way and has already traveled the path before us. When we hear His voice and remember the prints of the nails in His hands and feet and the mark of the spear in His side, we can know that, regardless of our many faults, we are redeemed by the sacrifice of His body and His blood. When we hear his voice, we remember that He died that we might live. We remember that at some future time we will see His face and bathe His feet with tears of gratitude. We will know Him then because we listen for Him now.

I need thee every hour,
Most gracious Lord.
No tender voice like thine
Can peace afford.
I need thee, oh, I need thee;
Every hour I need thee!
Oh, bless me now, my Savior;
I come to thee!

—"I Need Thee Every Hour," *Hymns,* no. 98

---

11 John 6:63.

WHEN THROUGH THE DEEP WATERS I CALL THEE TO GO—DESPAIR AND THE ATONEMENT

Come unto Jesus, ye heavy laden,
Careworn and fainting, by sin oppressed.
He'll safely guide you unto that haven
Where all who trust him may rest.

—"Come unto Jesus," *Hymns,* no. 117

For some reason, we think the Atonement
of Christ applies only at the end of mortal life to redemption
from the Fall, from spiritual death. It is much more than that. It
is an ever-present power to call upon in everyday life. When
we are racked or harrowed up or tormented by guilt
or burdened with grief, He can heal us.

—President Boyd K. Packer, "'The Touch of the Master's Hand,'"
Ensign, May 2001, 23

WHEN you were younger, odds are that you made plans—optimistic, idealistic plans—that you knew would invariably lead you through a happy life culminating with an inheritance in the celestial kingdom. In the first line of *Anna Karenina,* the great Russian novelist Leo Tolstoy wrote, "Happy families are all alike; every unhappy family is unhappy in its own way." Just as there is a similarity in happy families, there is a common thread in optimistic plans that allows me to sketch in broad outlines the mileposts you likely included as you anticipated a wonderful life.

Your ideal adult life would begin to develop as you completed training or education appropriate to your interests and abilities. Certainly, this education would not always be easy, but you would apply yourself and find great success in your studies, success that would confirm that you had selected a future vocation for which you were well suited.

At some time during or soon after that education, you would meet someone wonderful. Perhaps on first meeting or maybe shortly thereafter, an electric thrill would course through you, and you would know that you would join this special person in the most wonderful wedding the world had ever known. The Spirit would provide an unmistakable confirmation of your choice. By his or her words and actions, your perfect mate-to-be would clearly communicate to you that your feelings were reciprocated. It would be impossible to say who loved most, you or your future spouse.

A wedding would come in the appropriate June of this bright plan, a perfect wedding, characterized by transcendent bliss, and you would begin a wonderful life together. Children would soon arrive, beautiful, happy, healthy children who would each be a joy to both of you. What a wise parent you would be, how loving and insightful. Each child would listen attentively as you imparted wisdom and taught the lessons you had learned from life, the central importance of the gospel, and the necessity of high standards of behavior.

Thanks to your careful teaching and example, when your children entered their teenage years, they would have the strength to resist all the temptations of the world. As they matured, your children would be amazed at how insightful you had been concerning each of the challenges they encountered in their lives. They would always seek your advice and frequently express their heartfelt thanks for your loving guidance. In so many ways, each of your children would mirror the praiseworthy characteristics of both their mother and father.

In a carefully chosen vocation, the man of the house would find great success. Admired by peers, rewarded financially for hard work, his job would never be a burden but always an opportunity for personal growth and fulfillment. The woman might choose to work under circumstances that did not interfere in any way with her duties as a mother and would immediately be recognized as a valuable asset in the workplace for all the skills she had developed while raising her children and working in the Church and community. Or she might remain at home, completely happy and fulfilled in her domestic duties in a house that was always organized, peaceful, and filled with laughter.

One of the preeminent elements of your life's plan would, of course, be an active membership in the true Church of Jesus Christ. In Church service, the man would faithfully honor the priesthood and magnify each of his callings. Undoubtedly, his faith and righteousness would be acknowledged with many responsible Church positions. What a help he would be to all who came to him for counsel. Despite his important Church duties, he would never be unavailable when any member of his family needed him.

The woman would personify charity and service to others. Although never touched by sorrow in her own life, she would provide a great source of strength and comfort to those who suffered in any way. Angelic in her countenance, she would be the finest Relief Society, Young Women, and Primary president anyone had ever seen while always maintaining a perfectly well-kept and tranquil home.

As you matured, although your hair would change to a distinguished shade of gray, everyone would marvel at your continued energy and stamina. "Still sharp as a tack," they would say. Untouched by the aches and pains of others, you would continue to lead an active life, your comfortable retirement secured by careful financial planning throughout your life. There would be a mission, of course, perhaps two, interspersed with visits to adoring grandchildren.

At the close of this life's plan, no one would doubt that you were destined for the celestial kingdom when you died suddenly, painlessly in your sleep, just a few days before your spouse similarly passed from this world.

Is there anything wrong with any of these plans? Of course not. They are wonderful plans, beautiful and worthy aspirations. We all dream about similar plans and work to make them real.

But such dreams are incomplete and one-dimensional, never to be achieved without some departures from our careful outline. If the objective of our plan is the celestial kingdom, only Heavenly Father knows the unique individual path we must take to enter the gates of that kingdom. Regardless of the magnitude of our intelligence or spirituality, none of us knows what path our life will take.

God draws from a wider and more varied palette to paint our lives than we ever could or would. His reds and yellows are more vivid than any we could create or even imagine in our childish fingerpaintings of life. But cold deep blues, somber browns, and even blacks also reside on His palette. From time to time, He allows His wise and masterful brush to dip into these deeper colors and touch here and there upon the pathways of our experience. Disappointment, failure, weakness, illness, sorrow, error, and loss lend dimension to the landscapes of the heart with sober experiences that both balance and enhance His brighter hues. At times, layers of despair may extend over many parts of our painting.

It is common for people to feel great anxiety when their life's path veers from their life's plan. A cherished educational goal is not reached. Marriage does not happen. Children do not come. Health or wealth suddenly vanishes.

At such times, we may lacerate ourselves with blame. We think we have failed at an important junction in our lives and mentally extend that failure into all our future experiences. We may sometimes blame God. He has all power; He could have caused everything to turn out all right. He could have guided us or warned us so we might have avoided the disaster our lives have become. Under such circumstances, we may be at least partially correct about our own failure, but we are completely wrong about God's failure.

We may very well have made a foolish decision that resulted in our inability to achieve an important goal in life. But whether or not this particular failure was a result of something we did, there is a more important truth: While we live in mortal bodies in a fallen world, all of us fail at something, even something important. All of us are battered by the world, everybody makes mistakes, everyone commits sins, and all fall short of the highest standards and fondest hopes. "All have sinned, and come short of the glory of God."[1]

Our errors would be fatal to our eternal lives without the Atonement of Christ.

Our failure to achieve our plans for life may also occur even when we have done all we should. Particularly under these circumstances,

---

1   Rom. 3:23.

we may be tempted to blame God. "I've done everything I was supposed to do to raise a good child. I followed all the rules. Why didn't God do what He could have done to let my child be good?" We may not be that blunt in our words, but such feelings have a propensity to creep into our hearts during times of despair. Things did not work out as they should have, so someone is to blame.

Our mistake is to believe that God's focus and His goal for us match the details of our life's plan. Our Heavenly Father's focus, the reason He sent His Son to save us, is clear and simple: "This is my work and my glory—to bring to pass the immortality and eternal life of man."[2] That goal is what He focuses on. If admission to medical school is vital to achieving that goal for us, our hard work to prepare for medical school will be rewarded. If becoming a doctor is not important for our particular, specific personal salvation, we may or may not be admitted. If having children in this world is essential to our salvation, we will be given an opportunity to be a father or mother. If not, this great blessing may be deferred for us.

Of course our Father cares about our happiness. He cares more deeply for our happiness than for anything else. That is why He will give us the opportunity to walk whatever strange path is necessary for us to return to Him. That is why He has sent Jesus Christ to save us from the sins and mistakes and pain that lie along that path.

Any life that ends in the celestial kingdom is a great success. A life that ends anywhere else is not.

HOWEVER LONG AND HARD THE ROAD MAY BE

During his first speech to the House of Commons as the prime minister of Great Britain, Winston Churchill, with all the horrors of World War II looming, said, "You ask, What is our aim? I can answer in one word: Victory—victory at all costs, victory in spite of all terror; victory, however long and hard the road may be."[3] If the end of a long and hard road is a victory over death and sin and a reunion with our Heavenly Father, we will come to bless that road. Looking back, our

---

2   Moses 1:39.

3   Henry Anatole, *Churchill: The Life Triumphant* (New York: American Heritage, 1965), 90.

difficult path will make perfect sense, and we will understand how often divine intervention allowed us to continue our journey. While we walk the road, however, we may lack this future perspective. We may doubt its destination, we may fear for our ability to keep moving forward, and the rocks and barriers in front of us will loom large in our mortal view. All along that road, we need a Savior, and we have one.

A wonderful friend of our family, Becky, was paralyzed from the chest down in an automobile accident while she was serving her mission. That injury changed all the plans Becky had for her life. She would not marry when she expected to and would not have children in this life, yet she was one of the most optimistic people I have ever known. Of the physical condition that was to dominate most of her time on earth, she said simply, "Life doesn't always turn out the way you expected." She also said something that I have often repeated to myself and to those with whom I have counseled: "This life is the test, not the reward."

Becky's wisdom was a simple distillation of an important truth—from its very foundation, this earth was created as a test for each of God's faithful children. It is not the end of our eternal path, and it is far from the most attractive portion of our path. It is a test. "We will go down, for there is space there, and we will take of these materials, and we will make an earth whereon these may dwell; *And we will prove them herewith,* to see if they will do all things whatsoever the Lord their God shall command them."[4]

When I heard Boyd K. Packer present a talk entitled "The Choice" in the 1980 October general conference, I knew his message was important to me. I did not know how often I would need to return to my memory of that message in the years that followed. Among other things he said,

> I want you . . . to know this truth:
> You need not be either rich or hold high position to be completely successful and truly happy. . . .
> We come into mortal life to receive a body and to be tested, to learn to choose. . . . The choice of life is not between fame and obscurity, nor is the choice between

---

4   Abr. 3:24–25; emphasis added.

wealth and poverty. The choice is between good and evil, and that is a very different matter indeed.[5]

When Through the Deep Waters I Call Thee to Go

When through the deep waters I call thee to go,
The rivers of sorrow shall not thee o'erflow,
For I will be with thee, thy troubles to bless,
And sanctify to thee, And sanctify to thee,
And sanctify to thee thy deepest distress.[6]

The serious and chronic depression of my wife, G.G., has been one of the predominant influences in my life. Her illness began after the birth of our daughter and continued for twenty-five years. She was hospitalized several times and was treated by countless doctors and therapists. Neither of us can remember all the medications she tried to no avail.

I am a convert to the Church. G.G. was the first Latter-day Saint I ever met. When we met, G.G. was intelligent, vibrant, active, and alive. Even in her early twenties, she was accomplished. She had worked as an editor at the Hoover Institution on the campus of Stanford University. When she moved to Boston, she quickly found employment as assistant treasurer at Harvard University and then moved to an analyst's position with Fidelity Investments, a large and successful financial institution.

G.G. pursued a master's degree in international relations at George Washington University in Washington, D.C., and during her graduate education, she taught college economics classes. After our marriage, she was hired by Continental Bank, then the largest bank in Chicago, as the first woman to be trained as an international loan officer.

G.G. was spiritual and committed to living the gospel, always an excellent example to me in my own spiritual life. She was a wonderful teacher who had a marvelous and lifelong impact on the women and girls in the wards in which we lived. After our first child was born, she was a completely committed and loving mother.

---

5   "The Choice," *Ensign,* Nov. 1980, 21.
6   "How Firm a Foundation," *Hymns,* no. 85.

Then depression began to change her.

The illness did not appear suddenly. G.G. was the sun in my life, and the onset of her disease was like an extended sunset. First, the color of the sun changes, turning slowly red as it drops lower in the sky. Then, the horizon begins to take slices from that sun, one after another, and the sun grows smaller and smaller until it disappears from sight. In the sky, there is a glow, a memory of the sun, but soon that glow begins to fade. Shadows collect in ravines and behind rocks. Those shadows grow and spread, slowly covering the landscape. Soon the world is dark, then black, and a long night begins.

Those who have not experienced serious, life-threatening depression or been close to someone who has find it difficult to understand this illness. The reason depression is life threatening is that some people who are seriously depressed commit suicide. Medical researchers estimate that 90 percent of all suicides are related to "depression and other mental disorders, or a substance-abuse disorder (often in combination with other mental disorders)."[7] During G.G.'s illness, she wanted to die many, many times because her pain was so great. She has written about her experience:

> [You wish you could die because] you feel like the most wretched, horrible person on earth. You have everything anyone could want, and yet you are miserable. You would even welcome death to stop the only thing you can feel—deep, yawning, black despair. But you fear death because you know you will be damned by a God who must despise you for your inability to feel grateful for what you have and for your failure to exercise faith, hope, or charity. . . .
>
> When you have depression, the only thing that seems to exist inside you is a void so deep and so dark that you alternately fear for your life on the one hand, and wish for extinction on the other. You echo Nephi's anguished cry, "O wretched man that I am! Yea, my heart sorroweth because of my flesh; my soul grieveth

---

7   See "Suicide in the U.S.: Statistics and Prevention," National Institute of Mental Health, 2006.

because of mine iniquities . . . and when I desire to rejoice, my heart groaneth because of my sins" (2 Nephi 4:17–19).

Though you have not transgressed in any major way, you cry along with Alma, "O Jesus, thou Son of God, have mercy on me, who am in the gall of bitterness, and am encircled about by the everlasting chains of death" (Alma 36:18).

You tell yourself, "I am not worthy of a priesthood blessing, but if anything could cure me, surely it could." You seek many such blessings, but you feel nothing of the hope they offer. It seems the love of God simply cannot penetrate your breast. It is as though your heart were encased in a lead shield.[8]

This illness was not part of G.G.'s plan for her life nor was it part of mine. It was hard. Very, very hard.

G.G.'s depression varied in its intensity during those twenty-five years. There were times when its hold on her lessened and a shadow of the former woman became discernable to others. During those less-bad times, she could and did serve in the Church by teaching and acting as a counselor in ward and stake Relief Society presidencies. She was able to write and publish three books.

But the disease never left completely. Always, it was like an emotional and spiritual anvil, exerting a downward pull that required most of her energy to resist. After a period when she was less afflicted, the downward pull inexorably increased until it became too great and she sank again, struggling for life beneath the dark water of despair.

My own emotions often followed the rise and fall of G.G.'s illness. When her symptoms receded or she started a new medication, my hopes would rise. "Finally," I would think, "we're coming to the end of this terrible trial." I would pray and thank my Heavenly Father for her improvement, pleading for Him to allow her more relief, begging Him to make it permanent.

---

8   G.G. Vandagriff, Gregory Vandagriff and David Vandagriff, *Deliverance from Depression—Finding Hope and Healing Through the Atonement of Christ* (American Fork, Utah: Covenant Communications, 2008), 7–8.

Then, she would begin to descend, fighting, fighting all the way. She would drop and drop and drop back into darkness and pain. Sometimes when I came home from work, the house was silent and empty. I worried that G.G. had died. With a growing sense of dread, I would search for her, looking through every room, until at last I found her lying on the floor of a closet with the door closed and the light out.

Did the Lord forget G.G. during those times? Did the Lord forget me? Did the Lord forget our children? No, He did not.

I could not have survived, and G.G. could not have survived without the sustaining and strengthening power of the Atonement. The burden was far too heavy for either of us to have borne ourselves. We would have been destroyed without the Lord's help. I was not always aware of this divine assistance as it was being given, but in retrospect, the perfection of its timing and the extent of its protection is undeniable.

Despite G.G.'s illness, I was able to serve in Church callings much of the time. I was a bishop twice and a counselor in a stake presidency. I served on three high councils. As part of the Lord's kind protection, He provided me with wonderful spiritual experiences in connection with those callings, allowing me to feel His love, guidance, and inspiration as I worked to help others. As I observed the Atonement working in the lives of others, the Lord assured me that He was a God of miracles and helped me hold on to the possibility of a miracle for G.G.

Even as I wondered what had become of the life I had planned, the Lord sent me messages to reassure me that my life was taking the course that would be best for me, that I had not made some terrible mistake. I was called as a counselor in a stake presidency by Bishop Hales, now Elder Robert D. Hales. As he set me apart, Bishop Hales said something that was different from the blessings for the other members of the presidency. He told me that I had been foreordained to serve in that presidency.

I held on to that message tightly. It meant that regardless of the odd path that had led me to that place and time, I was where the Lord wanted me to be, in the place where I had promised I would serve before I came to this earth. As I contemplated this message, I came to understand that standing beside G.G. as her husband through all the horrors of depression was also where the Lord wanted me to be. It was often difficult for me to hold on to that understanding, and sometimes I would lose it. But when I needed it the most, a quiet confirmation would return. The message was not that the Lord was going to take away G.G.'s burden and mine but that He had not forgotten us and was walking beside us along a path that was often very rocky.

Just as I was called to that presidency by inspiration, I was released by inspiration. By unusual circumstance, the stake president was advised by our regional representative (formerly a priesthood leadership calling similar to an Area Seventy) to release both of his counselors after five years. Our stake covered a large geographical area, the president was told, and the burdens of traveling long distances in our callings were great. Since it was quite possible that one of his counselors would be the next stake president, it was wise to give us a rest, since twenty continuous years of such service would be a heavy load.

None of us had ever heard of such a thing before, but, of course, we followed this counsel. I was released at our stake conference. This was inspired guidance, but for a different reason than our regional representative had expressed.

Before the next stake conference, the wife of the other counselor was diagnosed with cancer and died. This wonderful, loving, and valiant man, my good friend, never recovered from her death and over a period of time lapsed into inactivity.

Before the next stake conference, G.G. was admitted to a psychiatric hospital in a distant city because of her serious depression. After this first admission, she would have many more.

Many years later, G.G. was still very ill when I was interviewed in relation to a prospective call as a student-ward bishop at BYU. The stake president, President Thomas B. Griffith, asked me about her condition and whether it would interfere with my service. I told him that I didn't think it would, and we spoke about her illness.

It was during this second time as bishop that I came to a greater understanding of the Atonement and how it applied to every aspect of my life. President Griffith taught powerful lessons about the Atonement. He asked that every talk and lesson presented in the stake be explicitly tied to the Atonement. The experience of including the Atonement in every message I delivered to my ward members and hearing the Atonement taught powerfully by these wonderful students changed my life. I shared what I learned with G.G., and the Atonement resonated powerfully with her.

During my time as bishop, G.G. came to campus with me when her health permitted. At times, she would have to leave ward meetings early. My prayers that I would be able to fulfill both my primary responsibility as her husband and my responsibility as a bishop were granted. But my prayers that she would be healed from her illness were not granted for the first two years of my calling.

And then, almost in an instant, she was healed.

G.G. had been declining, and her worsening condition was apparent to all who knew her. On one occasion, I had to hold her and help her walk out of Relief Society in our student ward because she was weeping uncontrollably. G.G.'s good friend Zina became very alarmed. She pressed G.G. to go to the doctor. G.G. replied that she had been to all the doctors and tried all the medicines and none of them worked. Zina would not stop and kept urging her to go again. Finally, G.G. made an appointment.

G.G. wrote the following concerning a prayer she offered during this time: "I finally said, 'Take everything. Do with it what You will. You can do a much better job with my life than I can. Whatever it takes, I want to belong to the Savior. I want that relationship to be paramount—to come before anything else. *I place myself completely on the altar.* I promise I will trust You no matter what happens; I trust You not to try me beyond that which I can bear.' I made myself totally vulnerable—a very frightening prospect for me. And I let go."[9]

On the day she was to see our family doctor, unknown to G.G., Zina and several other women in our home ward were fasting for her.

G.G. describes what happened next:

> When my doctor entered my cubicle, before I could say
> a word, he asked me what medications my psychiatrist
> had prescribed for my depression and anxiety. I told

---

9   Vandagriff, *Deliverance from Depression,* 27; emphasis in original.

him. He said, "Let's see if we can do better than that.
I found out about some new medications yesterday. I
have some samples, and I'd like you to try them." He
gave me two medications, both new.

Without much enthusiasm, I took both
medications that night. I had been down this road
so many times before, only to fail again and again.
Besides, antidepressants typically took weeks to work.
I had very little hope, but I nonetheless remembered
my commitment to the Lord and exercised a particle of
faith, as Elder Holland had suggested [in his April 2006
general conference talk, "Broken Things to Mend"].

The next morning, when I opened my eyes, the
blackness was gone. Beautiful light streamed through my
bedroom window, and a feeling of deep spiritual well-
being filled my soul. The fear was gone. The years of
blackness were gone. I was anxious to get up and begin
this new day. I couldn't believe the way I felt. As I sat
up, the world whirled around me, and I lay back down.

Side effects. Was I going to be able to tolerate
these new medications? At that moment, I decided
I didn't care if I had to live as a dizzy invalid, as long
as I could be emotionally and mentally healthy. I had
never felt this kind of peace in my life. I called my
doctor and he assured me that, in time, the side effects
would go away. Over the next three weeks, I gradually
began to feel better physically. Emotionally, I improved
daily. At first I was very tentative about the changes
taking place. . . . This was all new for me. As my true
personality emerged during that first month, I was like
a starving person who was eating for the first time in
years. Everything tasted wonderful. I was euphoric.

I spent more time on my knees than I ever had,
this time in tearful gratitude for the answer to twenty-
five years of prayer. At last, the missing chemicals had
been delivered to my brain, allowing the synapses of my
nervous system to function as they should.

When I went back to my therapist, he said, "Your family doctor was clearly inspired. If you had gone to a psychiatrist with the symptoms you presented, he wouldn't have put you on those drugs. I really don't understand how they're working."

I knew without a doubt that I owed everything that had happened to my Savior and to those who fasted for me. I had placed my trust in Him, and He had not let me fall. I was like a wind-up toy that had been fully wound, set in the right direction, and released![10]

At first, I doubted. After so many years, could something that I thought would be a part of my life until either G.G. or I died be gone? Was this just a temporary reprieve, a flicker of light in an ocean of darkness?

As the days passed, my confidence in this miracle grew. It was real. After all my disappointed hopes, this time it was real.

So many wonderful parts of G.G. reappeared. No one in Provo had ever seen the real G.G., and they were amazed. The one thing that has remained vivid in my memory of that time is G.G.'s laugh. It was a wonderful laugh that I had not heard for years and years and years.

ENOUGH FOR ME

I have not shared my trial to say that it was easier or harder than the trials others face. Elder Neal A. Maxwell has wisely counseled, "Only the Lord can compare crosses."[11] My trial was enough for me. It was not too much; it was enough. It was enough to change my heart. It was enough to teach me humility. It was enough to cause me to repent. It was enough to strip me of pride. It was enough to strip me of envy. It was enough to lead me to my Savior.

President Monson and other Church leaders regularly return to the Willie and Martin handcart companies in their general conference talks.

---

10   Vandagriff, *Deliverance from Depression*, 28–29; emphasis in original.

11   "Taking Up the Cross," fireside address given at Brigham Young University on 4 Jan. 1976.

I believe they do so not so much to teach us our history as to prepare us for our present. There is so much to learn about our individual trials from the handcart companies.

Not all of the pioneers who crossed the plains to Utah came by handcart. Not all of the handcart companies experienced death and cold and despair. But the Willie and Martin handcart companies did. Not all families experience serious illness, but ours did.

One of the handcart survivors said,

> I have pulled my handcart when I was so weak and weary from illness and lack of food that I could hardly put one foot ahead of the other. I have looked ahead and seen a patch of sand or a hill slope and I have said, I can go only that far and there I must give up, for I cannot pull the load through it.
>
> I have gone on to that sand and when I reached it, the cart began pushing me. I have looked back many times to see who was pushing my cart, but my eyes saw no one. I knew then that the angels of God were there.
>
> Was I sorry that I chose to come by handcart? No. Neither then nor any minute of my life since. *The price we paid to become acquainted with God was a privilege to pay, and I am thankful that I was privileged to come in the Martin Handcart Company.*[12]

While the handcart pioneers were on the winter plains, they did not understand that they were working out their salvation. All they understood was that they were cold and hungry and desperate for help. All they understood was that death was at their elbow, taking one after another from among their small group.

Did the thought that generations to come would honor their suffering enter into the minds of any of the handcart pioneers out there in the freezing blizzard? I don't think so. I believe that taking one more step through the blasting winds, living through the night to see one more dawn, was all they could think about.

---

12   In James E. Faust, "Refined in Our Trials," *Ensign*, Feb. 2006, 3–4.

These men and women did not know what the outcome of their suffering would be. They did not know they were becoming acquainted with God. They did not know that these terrible trials would lead them to the celestial kingdom.

And neither do we when we are traveling across our own personal wintry Wyoming plains.

That uncertainty is a vital part of the trial. Not knowing how we can survive, not knowing what lies ahead, not knowing how long a trial will last, being desperately afraid and despairing will turn us toward our Savior with an intensity that perhaps cannot be created in any other way. If we are to complete the journey that leads to eternal life, we can do so only by holding on to the Savior so tightly that we release our grasp on everything else.

I don't know if everyone needs a handcart experience in their lives to change their natures and make them fit for eternal life. I needed such an experience, and I know that if I hadn't needed it, a loving Heavenly Father, whose overriding objective is to bring me to immortality and eternal life, would not have given it to me.

Above all, our Savior is our rescuer, the One who will step in and save us. His Atonement has taught Him our pains and our limits. I am certain that He would like to relieve us from all the trials and sorrows of mortality, but a much greater, far more important rescue is always foremost in His mind. He wants to rescue us from mortal weakness in a fallen world and carry us back to our Eternal Father. As much as we sometimes beg for smaller rescues, if we will hold His hand even when He is not removing us from all our despair, a time will come when we will understand and have eternal gratitude for the celestial rescue He will provide when the fires of our trials have prepared us for the greatest of all gifts.

Considering the blessings that are at stake, is there any mortal price that is too much to pay to come to know Heavenly Father? I understand that some feel as if they are being crushed by their trials. I have experienced those feelings on some days, but I learned that I could endure more than I ever thought I could endure. Even during my worst times, if I had been offered a bargain that would immediately remove the trials but at the cost of not coming to know Christ, I would not have taken that bargain.

"And this is life eternal, that they might know thee the only true God, and Jesus Christ, whom thou hast sent."[13]

Always with the great challenges, our Savior brings us the help we need to meet them if we will accept it, and in accepting His help, we come to know Him. The more we allow the Savior to touch and guide our lives, the more carefully we listen for His voice and the closer we grow to Him; we want to hold tighter to His increasingly familiar and trusted hand because it is always nearby. Even in our darkest nights, we can reach out and know He is there waiting.

Let us return to a statement by Elder David A. Bednar, cited earlier, in which he speaks about the way in which the Atonement, or the grace of the Lord, strengthens us for our challenges,

> It is likewise *through the grace of the Lord that individuals, through faith in the Atonement of Jesus Christ and repentance of their sins, receive strength and assistance to do good works that they otherwise would not be able to maintain if left to their own means.* This grace is *an enabling power that allows men and women to lay hold on eternal life and exaltation* after they have expended their own best efforts [Bible Dictionary, s.v "Grace"].[14]

None of us could survive our earthly trials, much less the most difficult hours of despair, without the grace of the Lord Jesus Christ. We need a Savior for those times.

Angels Are Near You

Sometimes, when G.G. and I were in the middle of her long illness, people would tell us stories of miraculous cures that others had experienced with mental or physical illness. These stories were meant in the kindest way but sometimes engendered the questions, "When will G.G.'s miracle occur?" or "Will it ever occur?"

I do not wish to end this chapter on a note that will raise such questions in the mind of anyone who is in the middle of a great trial.

---

13   John 17:3.

14   "In the Strength of the Lord," 77; emphasis added.

There was an astounding and wonderful miracle that ended G.G.'s illness, but there were also miracles before that final one, miracles that sustained both of us while we were still out on our own frozen Wyoming plains with many miles yet to travel and that confirmed to us that the Atonement was at work in our lives, even though we couldn't see an end to our trials. The following is the story of one of those miracles.

One Saturday when G.G. was still very ill, my spirits dropped lower and lower. Nothing that I was capable of doing could reach her. I desperately wanted to help her but could not. As she lay in our bedroom, I was sitting in the living room in deep despair about her life and my life. I felt like I could not continue. I had worked so hard and so long, but I just could not do any more.

Our doorbell rang. It was a sunny day, but as I opened the door, the light seemed unusually bright and intense. Two people were standing on our porch, but I could not recognize who they were in the powerful white light. A thought instantly shot through my mind, *These are angels from God.*

Then my eyes adjusted. The two people were G.G.'s visiting teachers. They told me they each had felt concerned about her and thought they should stop in to see if she needed any help.

I invited them in and walked back to ask G.G. if she could see them. She said she could, and the two women went into our bedroom. They stayed for about forty-five minutes. I don't know what they said, but after their visit, G.G. felt better for the rest of the day.

Our Savior's grace manifests itself in so many ways. When G.G.'s strength and my strength were inadequate for the struggle, He sent two angels to our home to minister to us. Our trial with depression did not end on that day, but I understood that when I was too weak to go on, He would send help if I would come to Him.

Come unto Jesus,
He'll surely hear you,
If you in meekness plead for his love.
Oh, know you not that angels are near you
From brightest mansions above?

— "Come Unto Jesus," *Hymns,* no. 117

"NOTHING LIKE THIS HAS EVER HAPPENED BEFORE"—CHASTITY AND THE ATONEMENT

God has commanded that the
sacred powers of procreation are to be
employed only between man and woman, lawfully
wedded as husband and wife.

—"The Family: A Proclamation to the World," *Ensign,* Nov. 1995, 102

BYU student ward bishops are generally assigned a professor's office to use on Sundays and evenings for meetings and interviews. In order to convert a chemical engineering professor's office into a bishop's office, I put a book of temple recommends where I could reach it and placed a box of tissues right next to the chair where my ward members would sit. The temple recommend book and the box of tissues came to symbolize two options in the lives of my ward members.

Most often, I used the temple recommend book, explained the process of completing an online missionary application, issued callings, or talked about how the busy lives of spiritual and talented men and women were progressing. If the box of tissues was used, the subject was almost always chastity. The principal way Satan tempts faithful LDS men and women who are about to begin marriage and careers is through the miraculous power God has given them to provide bodies for His spirit children.

Before I move to a discussion of this topic, let me put chastity problems in context for those who have not had close dealings with a ward full of BYU students. The large majority of BYU students *are* chaste and clean before the Lord. Of that small number who violate the law of chastity, only a much smaller group does so on more than one occasion.

I do not hesitate to state my belief that the law of chastity is obeyed by a far greater percentage of BYU students than by any other large group of men and women of like age and circumstance. As some of the other chapters of this book demonstrate, most of the students are good people, very good people.

Chastity is unique because of one simple fact: the members of my student ward simply did not disobey any other commandment brought up in the temple recommend questions. During my three years as bishop and over the course of hundreds of interviews, only a handful of students ever spoke with me about committing a sin other than violating the law of chastity.

One more preliminary matter—neither in this chapter nor elsewhere will I betray my continuing obligation to maintain the confidential nature of private discussions with each of my former ward members. Any examples that I use will be accurate, but I will describe them in such a way that even the person or persons I am remembering will not recognize themselves.

As set forth in President Spencer W. Kimball's *The Miracle of Forgiveness,* the basic steps of repentance are

1. sorrow for sin,
2. abandonment of sin,
3. confession of sin,
4. restitution for the effects of sin, and
5. ongoing obedience to all the commandments.[1]

Elder Richard G. Scott suggested another step in the repentance process. In a conference address in April 1995, he said,

> I would add a sixth step: Recognition of the Savior. Of all the necessary steps to repentance, I testify that the most critically important is for you to

---

1   "President Kimball Speaks Out on Morality," *New Era,* Nov. 1980, 39.

have a conviction that *forgiveness comes because of the Redeemer.* It is essential to know that only on His terms can you be forgiven. . . . That means you trust Him and you trust His teachings. Satan would have you believe that serious transgression cannot be entirely overcome. *The Savior gave His life so that the effects of all transgression can be put behind us,* save the shedding of innocent blood and the denial of the Holy Ghost.[2]

To illustrate how the Atonement applies to a violation of the law of chastity, I'm going to include some dialogue between a bishop and a member of his ward who has a chastity problem. I'll use the name, "Cordelia" because I can't recall any former ward member with that name. Even though I am not naming a real person or divulging the details of an occurrence that any ward member discussed with me, the account in this chapter accurately depicts what happened with many different men and women in my bishop's office. While I am using a woman to describe the interview, the same pattern and principles would apply to a man. The law of chastity and the obligations that accompany it are exactly the same for both men and women.

As I have worked on writing this dialogue, I have not been able to recreate the intensity of such an interview. I think it might not be possible without risking an improper disclosure of confidential information. Of all the chastity interviews I held in my student ward, in only a handful did I have any impression that my ward member was minimizing the seriousness of their actions in any way. Most of the men and women who came to see me were fearful that their sins had ruined their lives and that the possibility of temple marriage and the celestial kingdom was gone forever. Satan was trying to convince them that they were irredeemably lost, that they should give up on their righteous hopes and dreams, that there was no way back to purity and peace. At times, it was very clear to me that Satan was trying to use their sin to destroy them. My responsibility was to reassure them, while not minimizing the seriousness of the sin, that

---

2   "Finding Forgiveness," *Ensign*, May 1995, 76–77; emphasis added.

they could be forgiven and to convince them that the Atonement would work in their lives.

Cordelia has made an appointment to see me after our Sunday meetings. Perhaps I've had a feeling she is having problems, but she has initiated the interview. I greet Cordelia and show her into my office. I try to make her feel comfortable by asking about her classes and commenting on that Sunday's sacrament meeting or a recent ward activity she attended.

Soon, there is a pause in our conversation, and the feeling changes. When Cordelia looks at me, the pain she is feeling is obvious. Tears form in her eyes before she says anything, and she reaches for a tissue.

"Bishop, I need to talk with you about something that happened on Friday night. My boyfriend and I were in my apartment. My roommates were away for the weekend. It was late. I had a big project due on Friday and was tired from working on it all week. I know that's no excuse, but we did some things we shouldn't have done.

"Nothing like this has ever happened before. He is a returned missionary. We have dated for six months and talked about getting married, but I haven't decided if that's what I should do.

"His hands went some places they shouldn't have, and I responded. It all happened so fast, Bishop. Then I pushed him away before we did anything worse. We talked about what had happened. We were both upset, and I was crying. He said he knew that what he did was wrong and that I deserved better. He apologized. I told him I was sorry for what I had done.

"I have felt so dirty and horrible ever since. For the first time in my life, I can't take the sacrament. I was supposed to go home today because my best friend while I was growing up is leaving on a mission and speaking in sacrament meeting. I lied to her and to my parents about not being able to be there. I couldn't bear the thought that my family would see that I couldn't take the sacrament.

"Bishop, I've never done anything like this before. When I was a Laurel, I promised Heavenly Father that I would always be worthy to be married in the temple. I didn't think that chastity would ever be a problem for me. It never was before. My family would be devastated if they knew. I always dreamed of being married in the temple, but now I'm not worthy to go there."

She stops talking and blots her tears with another tissue.

I reply, "You have done the right thing by coming to talk to me, Cordelia. Your actions on Friday night were a violation of the law of chastity and constitute serious sins. As you already know, what you and your boyfriend were doing could have easily led to even more serious sins. It is fortunate for both of you that it did not.

"The horrible feeling you describe is the Holy Ghost telling you that you need to repent. I'm glad you didn't ignore that feeling or try to minimize the seriousness of your actions. You responded to that feeling in exactly the way your Heavenly Father hoped you would.

"One of the scriptures that describes what you and I are doing right now is found in Mosiah. Alma the Elder is dealing with a large number of disturbing problems, including sins that are being committed by the younger Nephites. He has prayed to know what he should do as a priesthood leader and receives an extensive answer about repentance. The part of Alma's answer that explains what is happening with you and me in this interview is found in Mosiah 26:29–30, 'Whosoever transgresseth against me, him shall ye judge according to the sins which he has committed; and if he confess his sins before thee and me, and repenteth in the sincerity of his heart, him shall ye forgive, and I will forgive him also. Yea, and as often as my people repent will I forgive them their trespasses against me.'

"One of the most serious responsibilities of a bishop is to be a common judge in Israel for the members of his ward. Your behavior is something you needed to confess to your bishop as a part of your repentance, Cordelia. It's good that you came to see me quickly. Sometimes members try to repent of a serious violation of the law of chastity without talking to their bishop. They'll come in weeks or even months later and tell me they know they're not forgiven no matter how hard they pray. I feel sad that they have been weighed down by their sins for longer than was necessary. It has clearly been a heavy burden for them. These members begin to feel better almost immediately after they have taken the necessary step of coming to me to discuss their sins."

We will then talk in detail about what happened. I will tell Cordelia that I understand that it's difficult, but it is important for her to make a complete confession. A partial confession will prevent her from completely repenting, and she will find that she needs to come back to see me or another bishop before she can finish her repentance. I assure her that she only needs to talk about this sin one time with one bishop and that she won't need to tell every future bishop about it.

Let's leave my discussion with Cordelia now so we can discuss the importance of our physical bodies, including their ability to create new life, and how the Atonement operates to save those bodies.

WHY IS CHASTITY SUCH AN IMPORTANT COMMANDMENT?

We are accustomed to thinking about the negative consequences of the Fall of Adam and Eve. The Fall did bring difficult challenges for Adam and Eve and for us as their descendants and physical heirs.

One effect of the Fall was not negative, however. In fact, this effect was so important that it was one of the principal reasons Adam and Eve transgressed the commandment not to eat from the tree of knowledge of good and evil. *Before Adam and Eve fell, they could not have children.* After the Fall, this changed. Adam and Eve could have children and be parents. This opportunity to create a family made every negative consequence of the Fall worth suffering. Adam and Eve were able to obey God's commandment to be fruitful and multiply. Doing so brought enormous and eternal blessings.

After the Fall, "Eve . . . was glad, saying: Were it not for our transgression we never should have had seed, and never should have known good and evil, and the joy of our redemption, and the eternal life which God giveth unto all the obedient."[3]

The scriptures record many occasions in which God bestowed superlative blessings on the righteous *through their marriages and through their families.* After Abraham showed his obedience to God's commandments by taking Isaac up to a mountain to offer him as a sacrifice, the Lord stayed his hand and gave Abraham and each of us as his heirs a great blessing, "*I will bless thee,* and in multiplying *I will multiply thy seed as the stars of the heaven,* and as the sand which is upon the sea shore. . . . And *in thy seed shall all the nations of the earth be blessed;* because thou hast obeyed my voice."[4]

---

3   Moses 5:11.
4   Gen. 22:17–18; emphasis added.

When Isaac bestowed a blessing on his son Jacob, he said, "And God Almighty *bless thee, and make thee fruitful, and multiply thee,* that thou mayest be a multitude of people."[5]

In vision, an angel showed Nephi the great blessings that awaited him across an ocean in a new land. "And it came to pass that the angel said unto me: Look, and *behold thy seed,* and also the seed of thy brethren. And I looked and beheld the land of promise; and *I beheld multitudes of people,* yea, even as it were in number as many as the sand of the sea."[6]

One of the Lord's greatest blessings to Abraham, Isaac, and Nephi was children and the children of those children born into covenant marriages approved by the Lord. This is one of the most glorious ways the Lord promised to reward those men who worked so hard to serve Him well.

Elder David B. Haight said,

> The Lord . . . instructed, "Therefore shall a man leave his father and his mother, and shall cleave unto his wife: and they shall be one flesh" (Genesis 2:24), thereby giving sanction to the union of male and female in authorized marriage, which is heaven-planned for the creation of mortal bodies.
>
> The *earliest recorded commandment* to Adam and Eve was to "be fruitful, and multiply, and replenish the earth" (Genesis 1:28).
>
> We regard children as gifts from God, committed to our care for loving, nurturing, and careful training.[7]

One of the foremost blessings given when we leave premortal life and come to earth to obtain a physical body is the ability for men and women to marry and have children. Children are gifts from God, and *when husband and wife come together to provide that child with a physical body, they are working hand in hand with God in His great work of creation.*

---

5   Gen. 28:3; emphasis added.

6   1 Nephi 12:1; emphasis added.

7   "Marriage and Divorce," *Ensign,* May 1984, 12; emphasis added.

In a wonderful devotional address entitled, "Of Souls, Symbols and Sacraments," Elder Jeffrey R. Holland, then president of BYU, provided additional answers to our question about why chastity is so important,

> Sexual union is also, in its own profound way, a very real sacrament of the highest order, a union not only of a man and a woman but very much the union of that man and woman with God. Indeed, if our definition of sacrament is that act of claiming and sharing and exercising God's own inestimable power, then I know of virtually *no* other divine privilege so routinely given to us all—women or men, ordained or unordained, Latter-day Saint or non–Latter-day Saint—than the miraculous and majestic power of transmitting life, the unspeakable, unfathomable, unbroken power of procreation. . . . But I know of nothing so earth-shatteringly powerful and yet so universally and unstintingly given to us as the God-given power available in every one of us from our early teen years on to create a human body, that wonder of all wonders, a genetically and spiritually unique being never seen before in the history of the world and never to be duplicated again in all the ages of eternity—a child, *your* child—with eyes and ears and fingers and toes and a future of unspeakable grandeur. . . .
>   . . . I submit to you that *you will never be more like God at any other time in this life than when you are expressing that particular power.*[8]

We must keep ourselves worthy for this Godlike act. If we have sexual relations outside of marriage, we have committed a serious sin that denigrates the sanctity of this power.

---

8   "Of Souls, Symbols and Sacraments," devotional address given at Brigham Young University on 12 Jan. 1988; emphasis in original.

THE LORD BLESSES THE EARTH THROUGH FAMILIES BROUGHT FORTH IN CHASTITY

Through the scriptures and the teachings of modern-day prophets, we begin to understand how holy the act of bringing children into this world is, how essential to God's great work. Throughout all the history of creation, we see that mothers and fathers and children and families are central to how God acts and why He acts.

Consider how "The Family: A Proclamation to the World" speaks of husbands, wives, fathers, mothers, children, and the spiritual relationships created through our physical bodies in the following excerpts:

> We . . . solemnly proclaim that *marriage between a man and a woman* is ordained of God and *the family is central* to the Creator's plan for the eternal destiny of *His children.* . . .
>
> . . . The divine plan of happiness enables *family relationships to be perpetuated beyond the grave.* Sacred ordinances and covenants available in holy temples make it possible for individuals to return to the presence of God and *for families to be united eternally.* . . .
>
> . . . We declare that *God's commandment for His children to multiply and replenish the earth remains in force.* We further declare that God has commanded that *the sacred powers of procreation are to be employed only between man and woman, lawfully wedded as husband and wife.*
>
> We declare *the means by which mortal life is created to be divinely appointed.* We affirm the sanctity of life and of its importance in God's eternal plan. . . .
>
> *The family is ordained of God. Marriage between man and woman is essential* to His eternal plan. *Children are entitled to birth within the bonds of matrimony, and to be reared by a father and a mother* who honor marital vows with complete fidelity. . . .

> We warn that *individuals who violate covenants of chastity . . .* will one day stand accountable before God.[9]

A Matter of Spiritual Life and Death

As you read this, I hope the eternal importance of the law of chastity is perfectly clear. It is literally a matter of spiritual life and death. Violating that law is nearly as bad as beating someone with a club until they die. But our understanding sometimes lacks this clarity.

The Lord places us under obligation to obey all of His commandments.[10] However, the Lord's prophets and apostles have discussed three specific commandments with the warning that violation of those commandments is more serious than violation of others. When Alma confronted his son Corianton about Corianton's breaking the law of chastity, he said, "Know ye not, my son, that these things [Corianton's sexual sins] are an abomination in the sight of the Lord; yea, most abominable above all sins save it be the shedding of innocent blood or denying the Holy Ghost?"[11] President Boyd K. Packer has said, "Unchastity is 'most abominable above all sins save it be the shedding of innocent blood or denying the Holy Ghost' (Alma 39:5)."[12] President Ezra Taft Benson said, "The plaguing sin of this generation is sexual immorality."[13]

At one time, sexual sin was taken very seriously by society. Christ saved a woman taken in adultery from being stoned to death in an era when execution was the standard penalty for adultery.[14] We read about women being executed for adultery in some traditional Muslim countries today. However, in today's secular world, the idea that a man or woman would be severely punished for sexual relations outside the bonds of marriage has become unthinkable. Violation of the commandment "thou shalt not steal"[15] will result in arrest and

---

9   *Ensign,* Nov. 1995, 102; emphasis added.
10   See, for example, D&C 56:2–3.
11   Alma 39:5.
12   "'I Will Remember Your Sins No More,'" *Ensign,* May 2006, 25.
13   "Cleansing the Inner Vessel," *Ensign,* May 1986, 4.
14   See John 8:1–11; see also Lev. 20:10.
15   Ex. 20:15.

trial, but violation of the commandment "thou shalt not commit adultery"[16] is depicted as entertainment every night on commercial television.

We are constantly told that the sin which, in reality, is more serious than all but two others is not a sin at all. Given that sinning against the Holy Ghost and shedding innocent blood are exceedingly rare among the Saints, chastity becomes extremely important. When a man or woman violates the law of chastity in a major way, he or she drops into a deep and dark chasm where spiritual death of a permanent nature lurks on every side. These men and women need the Atonement more than they will for any other sin they ever commit.

Or Anything Like unto It

When discussing chastity in our day, that discussion must also include pornography. This is primarily a problem for men, although women can and do commit sin by involving themselves in pornography. It is a sin, a serious sin, and cannot be minimized merely because it does not involve the physical presence of another person.

Attending BYU does not protect students from pornography. The university takes many steps to prevent the use of campus computers and computer networks to access pornography, but most computer use occurs in off-campus housing, where the majority of students live. As with other violations of the law of chastity, there was more use of pornography than there should have been among my student ward members, but the large majority of both men and women did not commit this sin.

Repentance from violating the law of chastity through pornography includes the steps I have discussed and will further discuss in this chapter. In some cases, it also includes obtaining professional counseling through LDS Family Services or other sources. Because of the addictive potential that pornography possesses for some individuals, work with an addiction counselor may be necessary. Fortunately, the Atonement works for pornography just as it works for other sexual sins.

---

16 Ex. 20:14.

Repentance can be difficult for someone using pornography because they sometimes deny that it is a problem for them. Some will rationalize their use of pornography as not really being a violation of the law of chastity because they are sitting alone in a room and another person is not present.

The law of chastity is simple and straightforward. We are to have no sexual relations except with a husband or wife to whom we are legally married. The term "sexual relations" includes sexual intercourse, but it is not limited to intercourse and includes other behaviors, such as pornography and masturbation.

In Section 59 of the Doctrine and Covenants, the Lord set forth some of His commandments in simple terms. These commandments include the following, "Thou shalt not steal; neither commit adultery, nor kill, *nor do anything like unto it.*"[17] Adultery also includes fornication in this context.

What does "anything like unto" theft or adultery or murder mean? If I take a loaded gun and intentionally fire a shot so the bullet just misses another person, I have committed a crime and done something "like unto" murder. If I beat another person so they almost die, I have done something "like unto" murder. Pornography and the thoughts and actions that accompany pornography are "like unto" improper sexual relations and violate the law of chastity. Between two unmarried people, actions that simulate sexual relations or are calculated to cause a physical sexual response to arise in either person are "like unto" sexual relations and violate the law of chastity.

How Do We Repent When We Violate the Law of Chastity?

How do we repent when we violate the law of chastity? The principles of repentance are the same as for other serious sins, but the application of those principles is somewhat different and, of course, the urgency of repentance is great because the sin is great.

"How are your prayers?" was one of the most frequent questions I asked my ward members when they were having problems. This question is the spiritual equivalent of your doctor taking your temperature when you say you aren't feeling well. If you have a fever,

---

17   D&C 59:6; emphasis added.

you aren't healthy. If prayers aren't right, it's almost impossible for the rest of your spiritual life to be healthy. Prayer is fundamental.

The answer of someone who was talking to me about chastity was often, "I'm so ashamed. I don't feel like I can pray because of what I've done."

The feeling that we should not pray only comes from one source—our eternal enemy. Repentance requires prayer, lots of prayer, sincere prayer, prayer sometimes filled with tears. And this prayer should happen in a private place, a place where it will not be interrupted and in a moment where you have enough time to make it meaningful. A prayer begun just before you need to leave for school or work is not enough. A prayer begun late at night when you are exhausted is not enough. You need to plan a time and place for a good, long prayer.

It's often a good idea to say this prayer out loud. In this prayer, you ask for forgiveness for your sins. You don't say, "Please forgive me for the sins I've committed." You go through each sin separately, sin by sin. This will be very uncomfortable. You may have to start by saying, "Please forgive me," over and over, but eventually, you need to go through your sins in detail without glossing over or minimizing any of them. It is important that you feel deep sorrow for each sin and develop a powerful aversion to ever committing any form of that sin again.

This will require more than one good, long prayer. As you continue in your prayers, little by little, you will feel the Atonement begin to lift the shame. A feeling that you are forgiven will likely not come in a big rush, but little by little, like a long sunrise. At some point, the Holy Ghost will tell you that you don't need to confess each sin anymore, but that doesn't mean that your prayers should become less intense. The feeling of your prayers will begin to change as a sense of forgiveness begins to enter into them.

A second, fundamental part of repentance is scripture reading. Just like prayers, scripture study almost always declines in quality and quantity when a person is being drawn toward serious sin. You probably have felt that you haven't been getting much out of your scripture reading because your sinful behavior has driven the Spirit out of your life.

During the repentance process and for the rest of your life, scripture reading needs to happen every day. If you haven't been reading your scriptures for a while, start with your favorite parts of the scriptures, those chapters and verses that mean a lot to you. As you read, try to remember why those particular scriptures seemed to be so wonderful and meaningful in your life. You may find that these familiar scriptures will help you to feel some of the Spirit that filled you when you read them before you sinned.

After a few days, begin to include some of the great Atonement sermons in your reading. Jacob's sermon in 2 Nephi 9, King Benjamin's sermon in Mosiah 2–5, Alma's wonderful teachings in Alma 5 and 7, and Amulek's great sermon in Alma 34 are examples. In particular, you should study Alma's words to his son Corianton who committed serious sexual sin, in Alma 39–42. This is just the tip of the iceberg for Atonement teachings in the scriptures. As you become more attuned to the Atonement and feel it working in your life, you will find references to the Savior and His great and eternal sacrifice everywhere in the scriptures. Try to bring the words of the scriptures floating back into your consciousness as you go through your day. You may want to write an important scripture on a card or piece of paper so you can pull it out and read it throughout the day.

Because the acts of prayer and scripture reading seem to happen so often and are so much a part of our daily lives, we sometimes forget how powerful they are. In the absence of good prayers and good scripture study, repentance from an unchaste act may be impossible.

Let's return to my conversation with Cordelia as we talk about how to repent from sexual sin.

"There is something I want to warn you about for the coming days and weeks, Cordelia. When your spirit is in the process of healing, it is particularly susceptible to reinjury if you commit a serious sin. That's one of the reasons I asked you not to see your boyfriend again, at a minimum, until you and he have completely repented. You don't want to reinjure yourself and needlessly prolong the healing process.

"Pay close attention to what the Holy Ghost whispers to you, what He tells you to do and not to do. If you're ever in a situation in which you feel that the Holy Ghost has left, remove yourself from that situation immediately.

"I think the way you feel when the Spirit is strong gives you a preview of how you will feel when you see your Heavenly Father and Savior again if you are clean. If you are true to yourself, your real self, the Spirit will always feel wonderful for you, Cordelia. That wonderful feeling is a reflection of the person you really are, someone who wants to be clean and pure.

"By virtue of their circumstances, college students can become quite inward-looking and focused on themselves. They spend a lot of time thinking about 'my assignment' or 'my test' or 'my major.' Of course, you need to pay attention to your studies and be the best student possible, but it's important to add balance to your life by looking outward and by serving other people. In order to help you with your repentance, I would like you to look for opportunities to serve others.

"You can serve your roommates and friends. Also, our ward has ongoing service projects in which you can participate. BYU has a website that lists a wide range of service opportunities. You might pay close attention to the promptings of the Spirit to help you identify those whom you can serve as you go through your daily life and then follow those promptings. You may not know who around you needs your help, but the Holy Ghost does. If you ask for direction and follow that direction, He'll show you who to help. You noticed that I mentioned the promptings of the Holy Ghost, your spiritual physician. He loves to come and help you serve God's daughters and sons. When you're serving, your spirit is also being healed."

Cordelia voices her understanding, "When I help my little brothers and sisters, I understand how much God must love them because of how much I love them."

"That's exactly what I mean. There is one more thing, Cordelia, and then we'll be done for today. I would like to talk about a couple of things in your future as they relate to your present repentance. In my experience, people who have violated the law of chastity sometimes worry about these things.

"One of the most welcome scriptures for anyone who is repenting is a short verse in Doctrine and Covenants 58 that reads, 'Behold, he who has repented of his sins, the same is forgiven, and I, the Lord, remember them no more.'[18] In the future, after we die, we will come face to face with the Lord. When we sincerely repent, because of

---

18   D&C 58:42.

Christ's Atonement, our sins will be gone when that time comes to stand before Him, and that is a wonderful feeling.

"Some people have problems because of this scripture, however. They'll say, 'Bishop, I've done everything I can to repent and feel like I've been forgiven, but I still remember what I did.' I can understand their desire to forget, but the scripture says that the Lord will remember our sins no more, not that you or I will forget them.

"You will still remember what you have done, but because of the Atonement, it will feel different. Right now, thinking of what happened brings you only pain. What you remember now is a feeling of condemnation, a feeling that you are unclean. After you finish your repentance, the sting will recede from memory. It will be more like a warning never to do something like that again. You will understand that it was a sin, but the Holy Ghost won't make it painful for you like He is doing now. You won't remember your sin very often, and when that memory comes, you will be grateful for your Savior who made it possible for you to be forgiven. You'll feel clean.

"Let's turn to a scripture you are already familiar with that has a particular application to your circumstances. Ether 12:27 says, 'And if men come unto me I will show unto them their weakness. I give unto men weakness that they may be humble; and my grace is sufficient for all men that humble themselves before me; for if they humble themselves before me, and have faith in me, then will I make weak things become strong unto them.'

"Let's walk through that scripture step by step and apply it to you right now. 'And if men come unto me I will show unto them their weakness.' You have learned of a weakness, a problem with chastity, something you never thought would be a problem. 'I give unto men weakness that they may be humble.' You've demonstrated your humility by coming in to confess and talk to me about something that's very difficult for you to discuss. In your humility, you've demonstrated that being forgiven is worth the embarrassment of talking about one of your worst moments. You'll continue to demonstrate your humility as you pray for forgiveness.

"This next part is where the Atonement comes in: 'My grace is sufficient for all men that humble themselves before me.' *Grace* is another word for Atonement. The Lord is saying here that His grace will work for you, His Atonement will cleanse you as you approach Him with a humble and repentant attitude.

"And now comes even better news for you, Cordelia. 'For if they humble themselves before me, and have faith in me, then will I make weak things become strong unto them.' Your humility and faith combined with your Savior's Atonement will not only remove the sin, they will turn that which was formerly weak into a strong thing.

"If you had just stopped what you were doing, ceased violating the law of chastity, without going through the process of repentance, chastity would always be a weak area for you. You would have been susceptible to failing in that area again. Because you are willing to do what is necessary to be forgiven, which includes not repeating your sin, not only will chastity no longer be a weak area, but it will also become a strength for you.

"How is this important for you in the future? One reason is that there are some very important people in your future who you will need to teach about the law of chastity. They may be your own children. They may be a class of Laurels who are at a dangerous time in their lives. Because of your repentance and the effects of the Atonement on you, you will be able to teach about chastity with power. When you testify about how important this law is, the Holy Ghost will touch the hearts of those you teach and confirm that what you are saying is true.

"And you won't be a hypocrite as you testify about chastity. You won't be a hypocrite because you have repented, and the Atonement has allowed you to recover from your sin, to turn your life around, and has made you clean and pure before the Lord. Your Savior has rescued you.

"Cordelia, the Atonement is real. It is the most real thing in the universe. The Atonement works. It will work for you. I promise you that your Savior's sacrifice is more powerful than any sin you have committed. You can be clean and pure once again. You can pray to your Heavenly Father again without feeling unworthy. You can see your family without feeling guilty and take the sacrament again. When you meet the right man, you can walk through the doors of the temple on your wedding day knowing that you belong in the house of the Lord. You can do these things because you have a Savior. If you do your part, your Savior will always do His part, and you will have miracles come into your life because of His Atonement.

"Jesus Christ is a God of miracles, and He loves you. If you were the only person on the earth who had ever committed a sin, Jesus would have hung on the cross just for you. He would have bled and died so you alone could be saved, so you could return to the heavenly home where you belong.

"When you have a Savior like that, your eternity is secure if you take His name upon you, obey His commandments, and always remember Him. Cordelia, your eternal possibilities are wonderful, and they are real."

I will meet with Cordelia several more times as she goes through her repentance. Each time I see her, I will know that the Atonement is working for her because her face will become brighter as she is cleansed and becomes her true self again.

For Cordelia and each of my ward members, I prayed as hard as I could during repentance interviews such as I have described. The spirit of discernment with which the Lord blesses His bishops would tell me that the man or woman with whom I was speaking was a greatly beloved son or daughter of God and that the stakes were high. The Spirit was telling me, in so many words, "Bear down, Bishop. You can't lose this one."

At such times, I needed the Atonement almost as much as my ward member did. And the Lord never let me down. I felt His influence direct my words and saw the Atonement work time after time to heal these wonderful men and women from their sins and cleanse them until they sparkled and were wonderful to behold.

Though your sins be as scarlet,
they shall be as white as snow; though they be red
like crimson, they shall be as wool.

— Isaiah 1:18

"THE ALGEBRA OF AFFLICTION"— DEATH AND THE ATONEMENT

*The Lord restored his kingdom in these
days, with all its gifts and powers and blessings.
Any church that you know of may possibly be able to take
you for a long ride, and bring you some degree of peace and
happiness and blessing, and they can carry you to the veil and there
they drop you. The Church of Jesus Christ picks you up on this
side of the veil and, if you live its commandments, carries
you right through the veil as though it weren't there
and on through the eternities to exaltation.*

—President Spencer W. Kimball, *The Teachings of Spencer W. Kimball* (Salt Lake
City: The Church of Jesus Christ of Latter-day Saints, 2006), 5

*Now, concerning the state of the soul
between death and the resurrection—Behold, it has
been made known unto me by an angel, that the spirits of all
men, as soon as they are departed from this mortal body, yea, the spirits
of all men, whether they be good or evil, are taken home
to that God who gave them life.*

*And then shall it come to pass, that the
spirits of those who are righteous are received into a
state of happiness, which is called paradise, a state of rest,
a state of peace, where they shall rest from all their
troubles and from all care, and sorrow.*

—Alma 40:11–12

WHEN we are confronted with death, either our own impending death or the death of a loved one, we discover whether we *really* believe our religion. Is it the core and center of our being, a rock upon which we can rely or only an outward gloss, a shallow artifice, something we play at on Sundays without ever being truly changed?

Alma asked the question that we face at such a time,

> *Do ye exercise faith in the redemption of him who created you?* Do you look forward with an eye of faith, and view this mortal body raised in immortality, and this corruption raised in incorruption, to stand before God to be judged according to the deeds which have been done in the mortal body?
>
> I say unto you, *can you imagine to yourselves that ye hear the voice of the Lord*, saying unto you, in that day: *Come unto me ye blessed, for behold, your works have been the works of righteousness upon the face of the earth?*[1]

When the fact of death is before us, we must know, really know, that because of the Atonement of Christ, each one of us will come forth from the grave, and that our spirit, which never dies, will be reunited with our body in a new form that will not die. After this resurrection, our spirit and body will never be separated again. Because of His infinite and eternal gift to us, we can understand that we can pass through the veil, as President Kimball and Alma have described, and move forward through the eternities to exaltation.

Amulek, Alma's missionary companion, said,

> Now, there is a death which is called a temporal death; and *the death of Christ shall loose the bands of this temporal death,* that all shall be raised from this temporal death.
>
> The spirit and the body shall be reunited again *in its perfect form*; both limb and joint shall be restored to

---

1   Alma 5:15–16; emphasis added.

its proper frame, even as we now are at this time; and we shall be brought to stand before God, knowing even as we know now, and have a bright recollection of all our guilt.

Now, this restoration shall come to all, both old and young, both bond and free, both male and female, both the wicked and the righteous; and even there shall not so much as a hair of their heads be lost; but every thing shall be restored to its perfect frame, as it is now, or in the body.[2]

Here we see the Atonement operating in all of its power—raising the dead and exalting the righteous. Whether death comes as expected at the end of a long and productive life or as a surprise, even a seeming tragedy, the Atonement provides the ironclad promise of a happy ending for those who follow the Savior.

BILL

In our small ward in a small town in rural Missouri, I was a young bishop who didn't know very much but learned a lot about the Atonement very quickly.

I had been serving for only a few months. I had learned a little about conducting meetings and enjoyed holding birthday interviews with the teenagers in the ward. If I had thought about it, I would have said that being a bishop felt a little like serving as Young Men president, except that I dealt with adults as well as youth.

Most members of the ward were not wealthy in worldly terms, but they were very, very faithful. They were conscientious in their callings and wonderful at supporting their bishop. I learned that I had to be careful about what I asked the members to do because they would do it even if my request was not very wise.

I was blessed with excellent counselors. Bill, my first counselor, had served in the prior bishopric and knew the members of the ward well. He was serious about his calling, but I can still recall Bill's slow smile appearing as he brought a little kind humor into our long meetings.

---

2   Alma 11:42–44; emphasis added.

The first summer after I became bishop, we held a ward picnic celebrating Pioneer Day in the small city park. The sun was shining and the weather was warm, so all the children and many of their parents were splashing, playing, and laughing in the swimming pool.

On several occasions during that bright afternoon, my gaze went to Bill as I watched him play with his two younger children in the pool. Bill was enthusiastically involved in water fights with his daughter, Jill, and in boosting his youngest son, Aaron, high up into the air so he fell back into the water with a big splash. Aaron was scheduled to be baptized in a couple of weeks, and he dearly loved playing with his father. Tall and handsome, Bill was relaxed, the perfect picture of a loving father who enjoyed his children.

As the picnic drew to a close, everyone pitched in to clean up the remains of our festivities. I was carrying a basket back to my car when my gaze was again drawn to Bill as he rode out of the park on his motorcycle. Aaron was perched on the back, wearing his father's motorcycle helmet and holding on tight. I watched as the motorcycle went over a small bump. Aaron bounced and the oversized helmet rattled around on his head. I smiled as the motorcycle sped up, and Bill and Aaron disappeared from my view.

My family and I had just arrived back home when the phone rang. Bill and Aaron had been in an accident and were being rushed by ambulance to a hospital in a neighboring city.

When I arrived at the hospital, Bill's wife, Diane, was sitting near the emergency room with several friends from the ward. Bill's injury was very serious, and he was unconscious. Fewer than five minutes after I last saw him, Bill had rounded a curve on the highway that led out of town and had somehow lost control of his motorcycle. The police thought he had hit his head on a metal sign post. Aaron was also in the hospital and lay unconscious, but his injuries were not as extensive as his father's.

As additional ward members arrived, Diane asked if Bill could have a blessing. He lay so quiet and still, surrounded by an array of life-support devices. All the Melchizedek Priesthood holders gathered around the bed and lightly placed their fingers on the heavy bandages covering his head. Diane asked that my second counselor anoint Bill and that I seal the anointing and give the blessing.

When I give blessings, I focus all my effort on trying to listen to the Spirit, and I usually don't remember much of what I say. On this occasion, I only recall telling Bill how much his Heavenly Father loved him, and I blessed him that his doctors and nurses would know how to provide the best medical care. With all my heart, I wanted to bless Bill that he would recover from his injuries, but the words would not come.

Over the following days, I was frequently at the hospital. Sometimes I would receive a call from Diane or one of the friends or family members who were staying with her. On other occasions, I would simply feel that I needed to be at the hospital, and I'd make the hour-long drive. When I arrived, I always felt a good spirit and understood that it was important that I be present at that particular time.

Bill remained unconscious in intensive care. He lay so still under white sheets, only his chest moving up and down with the ventilator's rhythm. During the few months I had served, he had been such a wonderful counselor, a little older and much more experienced than I was, and always insightful about ward members in difficult circumstances when we discussed individual needs. It was hard to see him lying unconscious. I kept hoping he would open his eyes and signal to the nurse that he wanted the respirator turned off. I wanted to see him back with his family and to feel his reassuring presence beside me on the stand during sacrament meeting.

As Bill approached a medical crisis or his doctors attempted different treatments, Diane would ask that I and the other priesthood holders present give him a blessing. Every blessing Bill received was beautiful, and the Spirit was strong. But he was never promised that he would be healed from his injuries. I so much wanted to promise a full and complete recovery. I knew the words I wanted to say, I knew how they would sound, but I couldn't say them.

The days stretched on. The elders and high priests in the ward enlisted volunteers so someone who held the priesthood was present at the hospital day and night in case Bill or Diane needed a blessing.

After about two weeks, Bill's doctors conducted an extensive series of tests so they could be certain about his current condition. Several of us were sitting in a small, private waiting room with Diane when the senior physician arrived to discuss his findings. He showed us scans of Bill's brain with large discolored areas and explained that those areas had suffered extreme and irreversible damage. The doctor then told Diane that Bill would not survive. For the first time during this long ordeal, Diane lost control of her emotions and fell into the lap of a friend, crying, "Don't say that. Don't tell me that," over and over.

The life support machines were disconnected. Surprisingly, Bill kept breathing on his own for several hours, and our hopes for a miracle rose, but then he died.

Ward members surrounded Diane and the children with loving support, trying to anticipate their every need. While Bill was fighting for his life, Aaron made a complete recovery and, along with his brother and sister, was cared for by members while Diane spent most of her time at the hospital.

I had never planned or conducted a funeral before. As a convert, I had attended only one or two Latter-day Saint funerals prior to conducting Bill's. Fortunately, Gene, the high priest group leader, was an older man who had held many different leadership positions. He provided invaluable counsel on what I should do. I met the caring and conscientious funeral director whom I would come to know very well during my years serving as bishop.

Diane asked that I speak at Bill's funeral. I prayed hard about what I should say, and I still have my notes from that talk. I began with the following words: "There is only one message for a time like this—life is eternal. Your life, my life, Bill's life, is eternal. It did not begin with our birth and will not end with our death. Life is eternal." I spoke about the Savior and the Resurrection He would bring for Bill and for each of us.

Although the period between Bill's accident and his death was difficult for everyone involved, the time when I struggled the most as a bishop came afterward.

I didn't understand the Atonement as well then as I do now. I knew of and spoke about the blessings of the Atonement at the day of our death, and I knew of the central role of the Atonement in repentance, but I did not appreciate what the Savior's sacrifice meant for Diane and the children. I knew that they and Bill could be an eternal family in the future but not how the Atonement could strengthen and support the family through the difficult weeks, months, and years following Bill's death. Especially because Bill had been my counselor and my friend, I felt that I should somehow make things right for this family.

The burden was not easy to carry. Diane's faith was great, but I and others spent a great deal of time counseling with her after Bill's death. There were many details involving insurance and finances. Bill had managed all of these matters before his death, and Diane requested assistance in learning how to handle these duties by herself. Diane had not worked outside the home for many years prior to Bill's death, and she had to make decisions, carefully considering both the family's emotional and financial needs. The children had a difficult time, of course, and needed individual counseling.

We coordinated assistance during bishopric, priesthood executive committee, and welfare meetings, and many members of the ward provided countless acts of individual service to the family without being assigned, but I always felt that it was my responsibility and mine alone to somehow find a happy ending to this tragedy. I was the bishop, and bishops made things right. I worked long hours trying to return the family to something like the happiness they experienced at our ward picnic. Without a working knowledge of the enabling power of the Atonement, I spent my whole strength trying to save this family myself.

An increasing anxiety arose among some other members of the ward. Wives and children wondered what they would do if death visited their families. It seemed to me that I had to pull the ward together all by myself. As strange as it seems to me now, I never pointed the ward toward the Savior for security and safety. The increasing needs of the ward that I believed only I could address kept me away from home nearly every evening, most Saturdays, and all day Sunday.

This was a terribly difficult time for my wife. Bill's death made her feel insecure. She was struggling with the early manifestations of clinical depression, but neither of us understood this at the time. At times, she was suicidal but never told me. She did not want to burden me with her problems because of all the effort I was putting into helping Bill's family. G.G. felt that their needs were greater than her own.

Despite my lack of understanding of everything the Savior would do for Diane and the children, He visited them in their time of affliction, supported them, and helped them through this difficult time.

Jesus said to the grieving Martha as her brother, Lazarus, lay dead in his tomb, "I am the resurrection, and the life: he that believeth in me, though he were dead, yet shall he live: And *whosoever liveth and believeth in me shall never die.*"[3] Shortly after making this promise, Jesus called Lazarus to come forth from the tomb. He held the power, even before Gethsemane and Calvary, to raise Lazarus from his grave. After His horrible suffering and Atonement, He had the power and authority to call each of us forth from our graves to immortality and eternal life.

Even more importantly for the bereaved and brokenhearted, the Savior had and has the power to heal and comfort and strengthen those who weep for lost loved ones. Sometimes we look to the raising of Lazarus as the great miracle of the Savior, but His ability to bind up broken hearts, no matter how badly they are injured, is equally as miraculous.

Christ had the ability to help Martha, Mary, and Diane and her family. If I were to stand in the same situation as I did many years ago as a young bishop, I would trust my Savior more, and I would remind others to trust Him, as well. I would rely on the enabling and strengthening power of His Atonement to help all who were afflicted and point those who were in pain toward Christ for the very best assistance and comfort. I would understand that as a priesthood leader, I had important responsibilities to help my ward members and would carry out those responsibilities to the best of my abilities. But I would also remember that I wasn't capable of saving anyone from anything. I couldn't guarantee a happy ending to a sad situation. I could not transform tears of pain into tears of joy. Only my Lord and Master, Jesus Christ, whose priesthood I was exercising, could do that.

THE ALGEBRA OF AFFLICTION

When death comes suddenly, we need to understand that the person who has died has a Savior, that we have a Savior. We call some deaths

---

3   John 11:25–26; emphasis added.

untimely, but we understand so little about the Lord's timing. We feel that removing someone from their mortal life before they are old is somehow a great tragedy if we forget that the Lord, in His infinite wisdom, is also removing someone *to* the next stage of their immortal lives.

What about my counselor, Bill? Why was he taken from a wife and children in the prime of his life when they needed him so much? If he could have lived only a few more weeks, he would have baptized his youngest son. If he had died a few years later, he could have seen all his children through the teenage years that can be so difficult.

Bill had moved on to a place filled with a far more insightful ministry than he experienced in our small ward. He knew far more about eternal life than I did and didn't need my help. My job was to provide a mortal ministry to the people who remained behind. Heavenly Father loved this family. He sent His Son to take upon Himself the tremendous pain and afflictions of all families and friends who lose a loved one. The Savior loves those who are bereaved. Every anguished fear and each tear that traces a path down the cheeks of those who sorrow is engraved in His hands and in His feet and in His side. He helps the sorrowing in many different ways, both directly and through His humble servants inside and outside the Church if they will trust Him.

Elder Neal A. Maxwell reminds us that "the issue for us is trusting God enough to trust also His timing. If we can truly believe He has our welfare at heart, may we not let His plans unfold as He thinks best? The same is true with the second coming and with all those matters wherein *our faith needs to include faith in the Lord's timing for us personally,* not just in His overall plans and purposes."[4]

In addition to this insight, Elder Maxwell further helps us understand how important it is to trust God's plan for us,

> In life, the sandpaper of circumstances often smooths our crustiness and patiently polishes our rough edges. There is nothing pleasant about it, however. And the Lord will go to great lengths in order to teach us a particular lesson and to help us to overcome a particular weakness, especially if there is no other way.

4   *Even As I Am* (Salt Lake City: Deseret Book, 1982), 93; emphasis added.

> *In such circumstances, it is quite useless for us mortals to try to do our own sums when it comes to suffering. We can't make it all add up because clearly we do not have all the numbers. Furthermore, none of us knows much about the algebra of affliction.* The challenges that come are shaped to our needs and circumstances, sometimes in order to help our weaknesses become strengths.[5]

We cannot always trust in our own understanding of the death of loved ones, but we can always trust in the Lord, our Redeemer, and in His infinite love for us. In return for His infinite love, He asks us to entrust Him with our broken hearts.

"Trust in the Lord with all thine heart; and lean not unto thine own understanding."[6]

Suffering Pain and Affliction

The greatest light, the brightest light, the light that banishes all darkness, emanates from Jesus Christ, and He will always come to our aid. He has felt all of our pain, our smallest pains and our worst pains. There is nothing He does not know about pain and sorrow. He has atoned for *all* of our pain and *all* of our sorrow. Christ understands us so well because He has, in specific and individual detail, felt the fear, sorrow, pain, and physical and mental sickness of *every* one of us. We may sometimes believe that no one truly understands our secret sufferings. But One always does: "*In all their afflictions he was afflicted. And the angel of his presence saved them;* and in his love, and in his pity, *he redeemed them, and bore them, and carried them.*"[7]

In my mind, Christ's Atonement for our individual pains and sins is illuminated by the experience of the 2,500 Nephites who witnessed the Savior appear at the temple in the land of Bountiful following His Resurrection. These people had experienced horrible destruction, earthquakes, storms, devastation, and death at the time of Christ's

---

5   *Notwithstanding My Weakness* (Salt Lake City: Shadow Mountain, 1981), 67–68; emphasis added.

6   Prov. 3:5.

7   D&C 133:53; emphasis added.

crucifixion, followed by what must have been a terrifying three days of darkness while He lay in the tomb. I think that most, if not all, of the adults must have known someone who had died during the prior few days. It is possible that some of the children present were orphans.

When Christ appeared in the heavens and then descended to where the Nephites stood, He stretched out His hands and told them who He was. Then He began His instruction of this people by teaching them each a powerful lesson about His Atonement. He asked them to approach Him, one by one. Individually, they came forward and faced their Lord and Savior. At His invitation, each person reached out and felt the wound in His side and touched the prints of the nails in His hands and feet,

> Arise and come forth unto me, that ye may thrust your hands into my side, and also that ye may feel the prints of the nails in my hands and in my feet, *that ye may know* that I am the God of Israel, and the God of the whole earth, and have been slain for the sins of the world.
>
> And it came to pass that the multitude went forth, and thrust their hands into his side, and did feel the prints of the nails in his hands and in his feet; and this they did do, going forth one by one until they had all gone forth, and did see with their eyes and did feel with their hands, and *did know of a surety* and did bear record, that it was he, of whom it was written by the prophets, that should come.[8]

Mormon's abridgment does not record what Christ said to each individual as he or she felt these holy emblems, these physical proofs of His sacrifice for them. Considering how the Savior dealt with those who followed Him in the Old World before His death and Resurrection, I think He would have gently spoken to every person who came forward. In my mind's eye, it is not difficult for me to imagine Christ saying, "Benjamin, I received these wounds to pay for

---

8   3 Ne. 11:14–15; emphasis added.

the sins you committed when you were a young man. You did terrible things, and I felt the full pain of each of those terrible things, both the pain you inflicted on others and the pain you will feel if you are ever punished for those sins. I accepted that pain so that you would not have to experience it if you will humbly repent and come unto me."

I can see the next person coming forward and the Savior saying, "Rebecca, touch my hands and feet. Put your hand into the wound in my side. That is the place where a soldier stabbed me with a spear as I hung helpless on the cross. I understand the pain that stabs into your heart when you think of your husband who has died and your children who have forsaken you. Feel my side again so you realize that I know the despair that accompanies every tear you have ever shed. I was alone when I experienced your sorrow just as you feel alone when you experience your sorrow. Hold my hand again; put your finger on the place where the nail was driven through my hand. Do you feel now, deep in your heart, that with each blow of the hammer driving that nail deeper into my hand, I experienced the pain that you feel at being alone and abandoned? Do you understand that whenever you reach for my hand for help and comfort, it will always be stretched out to you and that all your pain is already in my hand, embedded there in the ragged scar the nail left?"

Because of the Atonement of Christ, death—our death or someone else's death—is not an end or a tragedy. It is a beginning, a step forward, a step upward in our journey. Our own death is a step upward, and if we take the occasion to draw closer to our Savior, the death of a loved one can also be a step upward for us. We each have a constant companion on that journey who has already experienced the pain we feel. If we will reach out to our Savior during our time of greatest pain, we, too, may come to know of a surety that He has died for us, that He has born our grief and pain and sorrow.

Through the teachings of President Thomas S. Monson as well as many others, we have become familiar with "Intimations of Immortality," the magnificent poem by William Wordsworth. This poem speaks eloquently of our birth on this earth and of our premortal home with God. With some small alterations, I believe that this classic work can also speak of another birth, a birth into the spirit world that we will all enter upon our mortal death, a place of glory and light and peace to which we may aspire because of the Atonement of Jesus Christ:

> *Our death is but a sleep and a reunion;*
> *The soul that rises with us, our life's star,*
> *Will have elsewhere its setting*
> *And returneth from afar;*
> *Not in worldly sorrowfulness,*
> *And not in utter nakedness,*
> *But trailing clouds of glory do we return*
> *To God, who is our home.*

—alteration of William Wordsworth, "Ode on Intimations of Immortality"

BILLIARD BALLS AND BANK SHOTS—UNDESERVED SUFFERING AND THE ATONEMENT

O Lord, how long wilt thou suffer
this people to bear this affliction, and the cries
of their innocent ones to ascend up in thine ears, and their
blood come up in testimony before thee, and not make
a display of thy testimony in their behalf?

—Joseph Smith, at the Kirtland Temple Dedication; D&C 109:49

Verily I say unto you, all among them who
know their hearts are honest, and are broken, and
their spirits contrite, and are willing to observe their covenants
by sacrifice—yea, every sacrifice which I, the Lord,
shall command—they are accepted of me.

—D&C 97:8

If we looked at mortality as the whole
of existence, then pain, sorrow, failure, and short life
would be calamity. But if we look upon life as an eternal thing
stretching far into the premortal past and on into the
eternal post-death future, then all happenings
may be put in proper perspective.

—President Spencer W. Kimball, "Death: Tragedy or Destiny?" *Faith Precedes the Miracle* (Salt Lake City: Deseret Book), 1978, 97

Macro Worlds, Micro Experiences, and Billiard Balls

Sometimes my world seems to be a billiards table where I am a billiard ball. When I am at rest, I can look around and view my life circumstances clearly. I can see other balls on the table, some close to me and others farther away. Because of my position on the table, there are also billiard balls I cannot see because my vision is blocked by intervening balls.

When the pool cue strikes me, I begin to move in a straight line. I can look ahead and predict where that straight line will take me, and my future seems very clear. Then I hit something, a glancing strike against another billiard ball that slightly alters my path. Next, my changed course sends me into a cushion that bounces me off in an entirely different direction than I had begun traveling. As I keep striking balls and cushions, my journey becomes more and more confusing, less and less what I thought it would be. When I finally come to rest, I am at a location far removed from where I thought I would end up.

There is, of course, another perspective on the billiards table, one much different from mine—high above the table looking down. The difference in perspective is profound. A bank shot looks and feels much different to the billiard ball than it does to the billiards player.

Speaking to Isaiah, the Lord said, "For my thoughts are not your thoughts, neither are your ways my ways."[1]

This is not a book about physics (and I would not be qualified to write one), but to understand some important things about living in a world where God's thoughts are not our thoughts, physics may be of some help. Sir Isaac Newton discovered laws of physics that I like because they are easy for me to understand. "For every action, there is an equal and opposite reaction," for example, makes perfect sense to me.

Newtonian physics explained the world for about two hundred years. However, as physicists developed more sensitive and accurate instruments, they began to discover problems with Newtonian physics. These laws could not reliably explain the behavior of all

---

1   Isa. 55:8.

objects. If the objects were very small or moving at extremely high speed, for example, the actions and reactions of such objects sometimes violated the laws Newton had propounded.

Based upon more precise observation and experimentation, researchers developed additional laws and theories, including general relativity and quantum mechanics, to explain the behavior of objects that did not behave as Newton would have predicted.

Although I have exerted some effort to do so, I cannot understand quantum physics. I accept that they are legitimate and real, but I am unable to connect the rules of quantum physics with anything I can perceive in my world.

For me, the contrast between the Newtonian world that is easy for me to understand and the quantum physics world that is difficult for me to understand presents a useful metaphor for the way we comprehend our lives and the things that happen to us. The "Newtonian" spiritual world is macroscopic—easily observable, the large view, the big picture, the view of the billiards player. While the Newtonian world is a predictable world, the "quantum" spiritual world is microscopic—not so visible, very specific, individual, and not so predictable for us—the experience of the billiard ball.

Applying the Lord's explanation to the Isaiah passage, the macroscopic spiritual world that covers vast spans of time is a place where the Lord's thoughts and ways seem not so difficult for us to understand. In the microscopic, minute-by-minute, day-by-day spiritual world, the Lord's thoughts and ways may often seem less comprehensible to us. This is a spiritual world where understanding will only come when the Lord reveals His thoughts and ways to us, often on an individual basis. This microworld makes us feel more like a billiard ball than a billiards player.

When we make decisions about our lives, we usually do so on a macroscopic, or macro, basis by anticipating the results of our decisions in the future. We save and invest money, expecting that the value of the investment will grow and that we will be able to enjoy a larger sum of money in the future. We sacrifice time and effort to obtain an education, anticipating that it will provide us with specific and important benefits in later years. We carefully and prayerfully choose a person to marry, expecting that marriage to this particular man or woman will bring us joy and satisfaction. We consistently and lovingly teach our children true principles and correct behavior because such instruction will lead them to successful adulthood.

On a macroscale, the principles that underlie such decisions are accurate and reliable. Out of a group of one million people, a very large majority of those who invest money will enjoy larger sums in the future. Most of those who carefully choose a marriage partner will experience joy and satisfaction in their marriage. Most of those who properly teach their children will see those children grow to wonderful adulthood. The probabilities are always in favor of the desired and anticipated outcome in the macroworld.

What a predictable place this world is on this macroscale! Righteous Nephites are blessed. Wicked Lamanites are cursed. Virtue is rewarded, while evil is punished. Faithful Latter-day Saints receive "peace in this world, and eternal life in the world to come."[2] Those who do not obey God's commandments do not prosper.

If applying laws that are reliable for all people throughout eternity always quickly and visibly delivered the promised results, it would be so easy for us to be obedient. We could effortlessly observe and understand cause and effect, action and reaction. Under such circumstances, we would readily gain a strong testimony of gospel principles. Such principles would be as obvious as our knowledge that eating ice cream brings pleasure and putting our hand into a flame brings pain.

Of course, our microworld, the one we live in from day to day, is not so predictable. Sometimes our experiences are improbable, falling to the smaller portion of the population that is, in the short term, an exception to macro rules and probabilities. If the odds of something happening are one hundred to one, sometimes we're that one, the exception to the rule. Principles of spiritual quantum mechanics may apply unseen influences on an individual or micro basis in ways we do not clearly understand. Sometimes our apparently small actions bring unexpectedly large and violent opposition.

Lehi explained some of these forces to his son Jacob: "For it must needs be, that there is an opposition in all things. If not so . . .

---

2   D&C 59:23.

righteousness could not be brought to pass, neither wickedness, neither holiness nor misery, neither good nor bad. Wherefore, all things must needs be a compound in one." [3]

Lehi's explanation seems counterintuitive. Our mortal understanding leads us to believe that a lack of opposition would deliver a better outcome than opposition could produce. Without opposition, we would reach our goals more quickly. Without opposition, it is unlikely that any one of us would fail to obey the commandments. Without opposition, life would be far more predictable and comprise fewer bank shots. Lehi's phrase "all things must needs be a compound in one" sounds to me like it includes a lot of bank shots.

Lehi propounds a quantum principle of spirituality to us—without opposition, we could never reach our eternal goals. True happiness can be ours only after experiencing and overcoming significant resistance in many forms. We gain spiritual strength only in the face of antagonistic forces that makes us feel weak and powerless. A bank shot may be necessary for us to come to rest in a more desirable place that we could not reach by a direct route. In Paul's enigmatic phrase, "When I am weak, then am I strong."[4]

No Pain, No Gain

Weight lifting belongs to a class of exercises called resistance training. In all types of resistance training, the body is required to move against greater resistance than it would during normal day-to-day life. By doing so, the body gains more strength than it could from normal activity. Weightlifters have long used the simple phrase, "No pain, no gain."

No athletic metaphor is perfectly applicable to a spiritual condition, but "no pain, no gain" provides us with insights into the way we are sometimes led to grow spiritually, particularly when we face opposition in all things.

For several years, I have gone to a gym to exercise. My workout routine includes both strength and aerobic conditioning. While these two forms of exercise differ in significant ways, the underlying

3   2 Ne. 2:11.
4   2 Cor. 12:10.

mechanism of each is the same—unless I am willing to continue to exercise despite some physical discomfort, I won't become stronger. No pain, no gain.

The process of growing stronger muscles is governed by simple principles applied repeatedly. The first principle is "exercising to failure."

Exercising to failure means that you must lift a weight until you cannot lift it any more. To develop maximum strength, most weightlifters choose a weight that they can lift for a maximum of eight to ten repetitions of an exercise. The first time you lift the weight it's easy, but that changes. By the time repetition nine arrives, the weight feels very heavy, and a burning sensation permeates the muscle. Despite the way repetition nine feels, the weightlifter starts number ten. During the final repetition, the muscles are exhausted. Without complete focus, the weight won't move. Slowly, slowly the weight progresses. The weightlifter can feel strength leaving the muscle even as the weight goes upward.

Finally, the weight won't move any more, despite maximum effort and total focus. At this point, the muscle is completely spent. If someone offered the weightlifter a million dollars to lift that weight just one more time, the muscle couldn't do it.

The weightlifter rests for one or two minutes while the muscle recovers much of its strength due to some miraculous internal biochemistry. Then, the weightlifter begins another set, another eight to ten repetitions of the same exercise, again to failure. After the second set, there is often a third and sometimes a fourth set.

By the last lift of the last set, the muscle is completely exhausted. The burning feeling is severe, and blood rushes through the muscle fibers to repair and nourish them. At this point, even resting for five to ten minutes will not allow the muscle to recover enough to perform a complete set with the original weight.

Then the weightlifter moves to a different exercise. Each exercise is designed to work a single muscle or muscle group. Most weightlifters perform several different exercises focused on a particular area of the body—arms, back, legs, shoulders. Arm exercises won't make the legs any stronger and vice versa.

After a few days' recovery time, the exercises are repeated. The muscle won't grow stronger from a single weightlifting session.

It must be worked to failure over and over. Most of the muscle's growth occurs because of the last two or three repetitions, the ones that are the most difficult and painful. If the weight is too light, the weightlifter may be able to lift it many times, but his strength will not increase as much as it would if the weight were heavier. If the ninth and tenth repetitions are undemanding, the muscle development that occurs only when the ninth and tenth repetitions are very difficult won't happen. No pain, no gain.

A weightlifter's muscles will develop so they are able to handle the weights used during various exercises. Over time, the weight must be increased to maintain continued growth. The purpose of the exercises is not to increase strength so that weightlifting becomes easy. The purpose is to increase strength so progressively heavier weights can be lifted. The weightlifter never stops exercising the muscle to failure.

As I mentioned earlier, athletic metaphors can't perfectly explain spiritual experiences, but our trials are often spiritual training exercises designed to change us, strengthen us, and encourage us to grow. We sometimes experience such opposition much like the opposition a weightlifter experiences. If the lifter didn't understand the benefits of increased resistance, he would not choose to repeatedly lift heavy weights. He would not choose burning pain. Resting feels much more comfortable, even natural, to the weightlifter.

However, the weightlifter knows that the muscles have far more potential. They can grow much stronger and larger than they are now. In order to do so, however, they have to work against heavier and heavier resistance. They repeatedly have to lift until they cannot lift any more. They have to become exhausted. Gain comes only after such experiences.

Think about the experience of Alma the Elder and his people when they were in bondage to the Lamanites. The Lamanite king appointed Amulon, formerly a priest of King Noah, to rule this group of Saints, and he was very oppressive. When Alma and his followers prayed aloud for help, Amulon threatened to kill anyone who prayed. And so the people of Alma continued their prayers in silence, pouring out their hearts to the Lord over and over again.

When the Lord responded to their prayers, He promised that He would free the people of Alma from bondage but did not do so immediately. Instead, He gave them a great blessing during their continued trials,

> And it came to pass that the voice of the Lord came to them in their afflictions, saying: Lift up your heads and be of good comfort, for I know of the covenant which ye have made unto me; and I will covenant with my people and deliver them out of bondage.
>
> And *I will also ease the burdens which are put upon your shoulders,* that even you cannot feel them upon your backs, even while you are in bondage; and this will I do that ye may stand as witnesses for me hereafter, and that ye may know of a surety that *I, the Lord God, do visit my people in their afflictions.*
>
> And now it came to pass that *the burdens which were laid upon Alma and his brethren were made light; yea, the Lord did strengthen them that they could bear up their burdens with ease,* and they did submit cheerfully and with patience to all the will of the Lord.[5]

The Lord answered the prayers of the followers of Alma not by removing the tremendous opposition in their lives, but rather by making them stronger so they could bear the burdens. The Lord certainly had the power to remove their burdens completely and would do so in the future, but at this point in the development of Alma's people, it was better to increase their strength so they could endure the opposition, overcome the resistance, lift the weight. At the end of their trial under Amulon, Alma and his followers came out of captivity as more physically and spiritually powerful people than they would have been if the Lord had lifted all their weights for them. The sustained bearing of burdens made them stronger, and they would benefit from that strength long after Amulon was gone. Continued pain, much gain.

Grace, the enabling and strengthening power of the Atonement, allows us to do far more good, to carry much heavier burdens than

---

5   Mosiah 24:13–15; emphasis added.

would otherwise be possible. We should not be surprised if life provides us an opportunity to demonstrate our increased power.

"Because thou hast seen thy weakness, thou shalt be made strong."[6]

REASONS FOR OUR SUFFERING

Not all classes of trials are the same. Elder Neal A. Maxwell suggested that there are three classes of trials: Class one trials are those we bring upon ourselves, either through sin or mistakes that are not sinful. Class one trials are true trials, but there is little question about their origin. We made a mistake and must pay the penalty for our error. We may revisit our mistakes, even years later, and reprove ourselves for our own foolishness, but in our heart of hearts we know that we have no one to blame but ourselves.

Class two trials are those that come to mortal men and women living in a mortal world. Somewhere within our body, a cell mutates and a serious cancer develops. We plant our crops, but no rain comes, and they wither and die. A child is born with serious physical or mental defects. As we age, our bodies begin to fail in surprising and unanticipated ways. The particular nature or severity of class two trials may be unique, but, so long as we don't seem to receive more than our share, we recognize that others face similar kinds of adversity, that no one gets out of this existence alive and rain ruins everyone's picnic sometimes.

Class three trials are personal and unique, given or allowed by a loving Heavenly Father who knows that it is time for us to learn a particular lesson, an important, exalting lesson. These are the hardest because there is nothing fair about these trials. They impact our most sensitive places. They come despite our doing everything possible to avoid them and do not spare those who are most valiant among us. Despite a life filled with faith and service, a wonderful woman never has the opportunity to marry. A dedicated and Christlike bishop loses his job and then his house. An obedient and hard-working missionary is struck by a stray bullet while he testifies in the ghetto and must spend the rest of his life in bed, unable to breath on his own.[7]

---

6   D&C 135:5.

7   *All These Things Shall Give Thee Experience* (Salt Lake City: Deseret Book, 1979), 29–31.

While the boundaries of each type of trial are not always definite or easy to discern, it can be important to understand as clearly as possible why a trial has come upon us. This prayer is not "Why me, Lord?" but rather a prayer to know whether this trial is being caused by actions that require repentance or not. Sometimes, not receiving an immediate and clear answer to that question may itself be part of the trial.

We have all experienced class one trials. We're running late, so we drive faster than we should and receive a speeding ticket. We make a purchase that we can't quite afford and then find ourselves unable to pay our bills on time. We watch a movie that is supposed to be good except for a couple of scenes and keep remembering those scenes when we want to forget them.

I have known some Latter-day Saints who view all serious problems as class one trials. They put themselves through unnecessary anguish by always assuming they are having problems because they have committed a sin or made a mistake. They urgently seek to know what obscure transgression they have committed so they may repent and remove the trial that is upon them. When a trial is not a result of any sin, these good people are frustrated, sometimes to despair. A fundamental tenet upon which they have tried to act in faith is shaken.

While we must be completely honest with ourselves and quickly repent when we have committed a sin (whether it seems to have present consequences or not), we must not automatically attribute the existence of all or even most of life's problems to our own wrongdoing. When we are counseling others who are undergoing trials, we must be careful not to search for an explanation in sin where there is none.

THE TRIALS OF A PERFECT MAN

The ordeal of Job includes a vivid illustration of how foolish we can be if we assume the presence of sin or error when we or someone else experiences a trial.

The first thing we learn about Job is that he was a perfect man. "There was a man in the land of Uz, whose name was Job; and that man was *perfect and upright,* and one that feared God, and eschewed evil."[8] While only the Savior lived a life that was completely free of sin, it is clear that Job had repented of all his sins and avoided most others. The enormous trials he would undergo were not the result of sin.

Yet, how did Job's friends react when trouble arrived? They told him that bad things don't happen to good people, and they surmised that because his trials were great, his sins must be great. When they looked at Job, instead of seeing the perfect man, they found sin where none existed and accused the perfect man of being a sinful man.

Job was understandably disturbed by his friends' assumption that he was receiving a just punishment for his sins. "My friends scorn me: but mine eye poureth out tears unto God."[9]

After an extended period of suffering by Job, as the Lord prepared to restore Job's blessings, He condemned Job's friends for their wrong-headed advice and commanded *them* to repent.

"The Lord said to Eliphaz the Temanite, My wrath is kindled against thee, and against thy two friends: for *ye have not spoken of me the thing that is right,* as my servant Job hath. Therefore take unto you now seven bullocks and seven rams, and go to my servant Job, and offer up for yourselves a burnt offering; and my servant Job shall pray for you: *for him will I accept*: lest I deal with you after your folly, in that *ye have not spoken of me the thing which is right, like my servant Job.*"[10]

Unfortunately, Job's experience with his friends is not unusual. When problems come into our lives, well-meaning people sometimes try to help by assisting us in discovering what mistakes we have made. In desperation, we ourselves may be persuaded that there must be some error. We anxiously search for a nonexistent fault, believing that if we can only correct it, our lives will become problem free again.

As I mentioned earlier, repentance is absolutely necessary if we have committed a sin. Even in the absence of sin, rectifying an incorrect decision may require us to bear the consequences of that decision or to work hard to remedy those consequences.

However, if our trials are class two—a result of living in a fallen world—or class three—suffering that has come to us when we are

---

8   Job 1:1; emphasis added.
9   Job 16:20.
10   Job 42:7–8; emphasis added.

innocent of wrongdoing—then trying to deal with those types of trials by repenting of nonexistent sins or mistakes is a useless and frustrating exercise and may cause us to miss the important lesson the Lord wants to teach us.

We all want to be able to exercise careful control over our lives. When we are experiencing great pain, we want to believe that we have it within our power to diminish or remove that pain. It is very difficult for some to believe that faithfully living the gospel will not always protect them from serious trials. On an intellectual level, they may concede that this is a possibility, but emotionally they deny it. Good things happen to good people. Bad things happen to bad people.

The answer to this conflict is that *we can always control our lives on a macro level.* We *do* have control over our eternal destiny. Because of the Atonement, if we seek to enter the celestial kingdom and take the steps necessary to achieve that goal, we can look forward to our miraculous reward *with perfect confidence.* If we do our part, the Savior will *always* do His part, and we *can* return to our heavenly home. *He is perfectly reliable.* The steps we must take are not easy, but they are achievable, and the outcome is certain. This level of cause and effect is a Newtonian level of spiritual truth—understandable, predictable, and dependable.

On a micro level, however, in our day-to-day and week-to-week and even year-to-year lives, we have less power. It seems that the more entangled with mortality an issue is, the less we are able to manage it. We may have precise control over the location of our future eternal home while we cannot pay the mortgage on our earthly home. We may be confident of enjoying an eternal marriage without knowing who we will marry or even if we will marry in this life. We may have perfect faith that a baby daughter will be with us forever without knowing whether she will survive the night. In these shorter, mortal time frames, our world feels governed by quantum forces, full of surprises and unpredictability, where cause and effect aren't clearly correlated.

Why must this be so? Because the Lord loves us. Because unless we turn to Him with all our hearts and put all trust in Him without reservation, He cannot save us. We must give everything we have, draw as close as possible to Him in order for His Atonement to change us enough so we can return to our Heavenly Father. If we had complete control over all aspects of our earthly lives, we would be unlikely to turn to our Savior with sufficient intensity. In fact, we would be in danger of living out mortality as contented natural men and women, forgetting Him and foregoing our opportunity for eternal salvation.

We cannot save ourselves. No matter how hard we try or how long we work, we just can't do it. Whether we wish to be saved through all eternity or to be saved during a dark and terrible hour, our only salvation is in Christ.

A CHASTENING LOVE

"Verily, thus saith the Lord *unto you whom I love,* and *whom I love I also chasten* that their sins may be forgiven, for *with the chastisement I prepare a way for their deliverance in all things out of temptation,* and I have loved you—Wherefore, *ye must needs be chastened* and stand rebuked before my face."[11]

What does "chasten" mean?

We understand that chastening sometimes includes punishment, but it is a much larger concept. In its broader sense, it is one of the most important ways the Lord helps us to grow. The definition of *chasten* includes the following:

- To correct by punishment or reproof; take to task
- To inflict suffering upon for purposes of moral improvement
- To restrain; subdue
- To rid of excess; refine or purify

Synonyms for *chasten* include:

- *Discipline, punish*
- *Humble*
- *Purify*
- *Simplify*

The Apostle Paul had personal experience with the Lord's chastisement and learned its true meaning. To the Hebrews, he wrote:

---

11   D&C 95:1–2; emphasis added.

And ye have forgotten the exhortation which speaketh
unto you *as unto children,* My son, *despise not thou the
chastening of the Lord,* nor faint when thou art rebuked
of him:

For *whom the Lord loveth he chasteneth,* and
scourgeth every son whom he receiveth.

If ye endure chastening, *God dealeth with you as with
sons; for what son is he whom the father chasteneth not?*

But if ye be without chastisement, whereof all are
partakers, then are ye bastards, and not sons.

Furthermore we have had fathers of our flesh
which corrected us, and we gave them reverence: shall
we not much rather be in subjection unto the Father
of spirits, and live?

For they verily for a few days chastened us after
their own pleasure; but *he for our profit,* that we might
be *partakers of his holiness.*

Now *no chastening for the present seemeth to be
joyous,* but grievous: nevertheless *afterward it yieldeth
the peaceable fruit of righteousness* unto them which are
exercised thereby.[12]

If we are becoming refined and purified through chastening,
should we resent that chastening experience, even if it is unpleasant?
Proverbs records simply, "My son, despise not the chastening of the
Lord; neither be weary of his correction: For *whom the Lord loveth he
correcteth; even as a father the son in whom he delighteth.* "[13]

The comparison of God's chastening to the guidance a parent
provides a child is illuminating. When we teach a small child over
and over to be reverent in church, does the child know why it is
important to stop making noise? When our young daughter wanders
into a busy street, does she understand why we snatch her quickly,
startling her and scolding her, to keep her from harm? When our
son cries after we decline to give him ice cream for breakfast, lunch,

---

12   Heb. 12:5–11; emphasis added.
13   Prov. 3:11–12; emphasis added.

dinner, and a bedtime snack, does he comprehend the reasons why we deprive him of this delicious food? Do we ever teach one child in a different manner than we teach another, considering the particular characteristics of each individual?

As loving parents, we do many things that our children do not understand, take actions that may even make them angry or sad in order to instruct them in correct principles and to protect them from harm. Sometimes only after they reach adulthood do our children recognize that the discomfort and deprivation they perceived and the punishments they received were vital to their health and welfare. In most cases, a child receives correction and enforced guidance long before he or she fully comprehends the principle underlying the parent's teachings. Indeed, a child may not even be capable of learning the principle until he or she has practiced its associated behavior. We hope our grown children come to know that they are better adults as a result of the ways we instructed them in their formative years.

When do we need correction from our Heavenly Father? How is that correction best delivered? When do we need guidance? When do we need purification? When do we need humility? When are we ready to be refined? As children of God, can we claim to know the answers to these eternally important questions? The more fragmentary our knowledge, the more important it is that our trust in our Father and our Savior be complete.

Through a broader understanding of the varying reasons that the Lord chastens us, we can come to a clearer understanding and acceptance of the full range of trials that we each encounter.

When we commit sins, we may receive correction by punishment from our Heavenly Father. What is the purpose of that correction? It is to soften our hearts and prompt us to repent and to turn away from sin and back toward our Heavenly Father. Does this punishment include paying the price for our sin in this world? I don't believe that it does because even the worst mortal punishment does not reach the level of the penalty meted out by divine justice if we fail to repent. Chastisement—correction by punishment—is calculated to bring us back under the protection of the Atonement so we do not ever have to pay the full price of our sins.

Other trials, unearned by our own sinful behavior, fall under the purifying, subduing, and refining aspects of the Lord's chastening.

WHY?

Some of the most difficult trials are initiated through the actions of others. A moment's inattention by a driver cripples a child and begins a lifelong trial for the child, his parents, his brothers, and his sisters. An abusive parent damages a child, and that child in turn passes the abuse and pain down to another generation. Wonderful parents lovingly and carefully rear a son or daughter who strays far away from the principles received in childhood and who responds to parental love with rebellion, insult, and anger. An adulterous father focused on satisfying his own lusts destroys the peace and security of an innocent wife and children. A terrorist bomb mutilates the bodies of innocents and hurls their minds into a world of ceaseless fear.

The existence of such experiences leads some to doubt. "If there is a God," they ask, "why does He allow such terrible things to happen?" Such doubt may lead to criticism of a loving Father. "A just God would have prevented this tragedy from occurring. God must be capricious, distant, and uncaring to permit the world to be so full of pain."

This earth is first and foremost an accelerated learning environment wherein all of God's children are given the opportunity to grow at a rate much faster than they can appreciate before they arrive here (and sometimes even in the middle of the learning process). For those who do not understand its true nature, a spiritual classroom seems capricious and unreasonable, particularly if they enter that classroom without understanding that they will receive final examinations in a variety of subjects and in a variety of ways. They have forgotten that they signed up for the classes and the examinations as the capstone to thousands of years of prior education before they came to earth.

While each of us commits sin and must pass the part of our examination relating to repentance, there are other aspects of the examination. These different aspects assess how well we remember the love of Christ when we suffer without fault. We may understand the Atonement in theory, but will we really apply its healing and strengthening power in practice when distracting disaster and despair enter our lives?

In a multiple-choice question, can we identify the Holy Ghost and distinguish His direction from a host of competing voices? An essay question asks us to explain how the redemptive power of Christ can overcome all obstacles and is more powerful than any sorrow we may encounter in mortality. This question asks us to provide examples from our own experience.

Without affliction, we would not have the opportunity to choose God when that choice is most difficult. We are capable of making that choice, but we have to prove that we will make such a choice under every circumstance. We are confronted with a wide variety of experiences, including some ghastly ones, and then asked, "Where is your heart, really? What name is written on it? Who do you choose?" When we choose God in the most adverse conditions, we are chosen in return: "I have chosen thee in the furnace of affliction."[14]

Elder Maxwell has written:

> To err by having naive expectations concerning the purposes of life is to err everlastingly. Life is neither a pleasure palace through whose narrow portals we pass briefly, laughingly, and heedlessly before extinction, nor a cruel predicament in an immense and sad wasteland. It is the middle (but briefest) and proving estate . . . in man's carefully constructed continuum of experience.
>
> One day we will understand fully how complete our commitment was in our first estate in accepting the very conditions of challenge in our second estate about which we sometimes complain in this school of stress. Our collective and personal premortal promises will then be laid clearly before us.[15]

TRAGEDY OR DESTINY?

Class two trials come to all who live as mortal beings in a mortal world and are with us on a continual basis. A collection of these trials is an automatic part of every life.

---

14   Isaiah 48:10; see also 1 Nephi 20:10.

15   *All These Things*, 47.

If we live in a sunny desert, we may be tried by drought. If we live in a lush forest, we may be tried by floods. The young may be tried by impulsive behavior and raging hormones, the old by declining physical capabilities and the melancholy of departed family and friends. The poor may experience the constantly grinding worry of the next meal, while the rich face the moral and spiritual destitution that accompanies self-satisfaction and disdainful pride.

It is impossible for any person to travel through life *without being tested.* The greatest man ever to walk the earth endured the greatest of all tests.

In a discourse entitled "Tragedy or Destiny?" President Spencer W. Kimball asked and answered a question as old as tears:

> Could the Lord have prevented [all] tragedies? The answer is yes. The Lord is omnipotent, with all power to control our lives, save us pain, prevent all accidents, drive all planes and cars, feed us, protect us, save us from labor, effort, sickness, even from death, if he will. But he will not.
>
> We should be able to understand this, because we can realize how unwise it would be for us to shield our children from all effort, from disappointments, temptations, sorrows, and suffering. . . .
>
> Is there not wisdom in his giving us trials that we might rise above them, responsibilities that we might achieve, work to harden our muscles, sorrows to try our souls? Are we not exposed to temptations to test our strength, sickness that we might learn patience, death that we might be immortalized and glorified?[16]

The immense and unquenchable love of our Heavenly Father does not include a promise that we will not suffer sorrow, pain, despair, and death in our lives directly or through the lives of those we love. Instead of a lack of pain, our Father promises us a Savior who will bear our grief and carry our sorrows.[17] In ways we do not fully understand, the universal impediments of mortality allow our Heavenly Father to keep

---

16   *Faith Precedes the Miracle*, 178.

17   See Isa. 53:4, Mosiah 14:4.

His magnificent promises, to complete His work and magnify His glory, to bestow immortality and eternal life upon us.[18]

He is a God who loves His children deeply. He would not allow any sorrow, harm, or injury to come upon us unless it were necessary to bring us home. When we are back in our heavenly home, if we think to ask, "Was there no other way?" He will assure us, "There was no other way." When we have faithfully endured all things and feel His arms around us again, we will have a perfect understanding why eternal joy is worth a moment's earthly pain.

If we are faithful, in a distant time and a better place, we too will have spirit children. We will love them with a greater love than we can possibly imagine today. We may teach them of our wondrous Savior, Jesus Christ, and how His Atonement has saved us and made it possible for us to be their parents. Because we love our spirit children, we will want to teach them about eternal truths and all other things necessary for them to grow up strong and good, everything they will need to know when they leave home. Can we effectively teach anything that we ourselves have not learned? Can we assure our children that with the help of their Savior they can overcome all trials if we do not ourselves have such a personal testimony? If we have to pay a price to plant such a testimony in our hearts, is there any price too great?

THE EXCELLENCY OF THE KNOWLEDGE OF CHRIST

Near the end of his terribly difficult life, Paul wrote a letter to the Philippians. He was in bondage in Rome, the city where he would be martyred. Unlike his letters to the Saints in other cities, Paul did not address any significant problems nor did he call the Philippians to repentance. He was an old man who had lived a hard and trying life. He spoke to the Philippians about his life and his Savior. At times, Paul seemed to be hanging between this life and the next. For me, among the most Christlike words Paul produced were those about suffering, his individual suffering, and how he was able to transcend that suffering,

> Christ shall be magnified in my body, whether it be
> by life, or by death. For to me *to live is Christ,* and to

---

18   See Moses 1:39.

die is gain. But if I live in the flesh, this is the fruit of my labour: yet what I shall choose I wot not. For I am in a strait betwixt two, having a desire to depart, and to be with Christ; which is far better: Nevertheless to abide in the flesh is more needful for you. . . . For unto you it is given in the behalf of Christ, *not only to believe on him, but also to suffer for his sake.*[19]

I count all things but loss for *the excellency of the knowledge of Christ Jesus my Lord: for whom I have suffered the loss of all things,* and do count them but dung, *that I may win Christ, And be found in him,* not having mine own righteousness . . . but that which is through the faith of Christ, the righteousness which is of God by faith: *That I may know him, and the power of his resurrection, and the fellowship of his sufferings,* being made conformable unto his death; If by any means I might attain unto the resurrection of the dead. [20]

Paul is perfectly submissive to his Savior. He vividly perceives the wondrous blessings that await him beyond the grave but is completely content to remain where he can minister to the Saints in Philippi so long as he lives. Paul wants whatever Christ wants.

Few of us would desire to trade trials with Paul. For about thirty years, he has been almost continuously traveling on his difficult missions. His back carries deep, painful scars from being beaten nearly to death over and over. He has been bound in chains, imprisoned, and shipwrecked in violent storms. He has suffered a "thorn in the flesh" so severe that he, an Apostle, has prayed fervently for its release, and, yet, his request has not been granted.[21] Enemies intent on his death have surrounded him almost constantly. He has battled the worst of Satan's evil influences to nurture the immature converts in the Church of Jesus Christ. During all the years since his conversion, he has been scorned and abused because of his beliefs.

---

19   Philip. 1:20–24, 29; emphasis added.

20   Philip. 3:8–11; emphasis added.

21   See 2 Cor. 12:7–10.

It is not possible to compare crosses, but Paul has suffered more afflictions than I have, more afflictions than the people I know have suffered. And, yet, Paul is perfectly at peace. Despite the certainty that more trials await him, he is calm, confident, and secure. His difficult personal experiences allow him to promise, "the peace of God, which passeth all understanding, shall keep your hearts and minds through Christ Jesus."[22]

The only response that allowed Paul to survive his terrible ordeals was a steadfast submission to and trust in Jesus Christ. Only through such a relationship, such an "excellent knowledge" of the grace of the Savior, could Paul receive so much strength and comfort. Paul was willing to open himself up to that grace, and it poured into him—an infinite and eternal wellspring of power and love.

The trials Paul experienced were far beyond those attendant to mortal life on earth. They were an individualized course of instruction and tempering particular to him. All faithful Saints will experience some such tests of faith and commitment, tailored to their personal capacities and needs. And these will be real tests, not pretend tests. Grades will be given.

Elder Maxwell said, "When we take Jesus' yoke upon us, this admits us eventually to what Paul called the 'fellowship of [Christ's] sufferings' (Philippians 3:10). Whether illness or aloneness, injustice or rejection . . . our comparatively small-scale sufferings, if we are meek, will sink into the very marrow of the soul. We then better appreciate not only Jesus' sufferings for us but also His matchless character, moving us to greater adoration and even emulation."[23]

If we are to respond to tribulation by either growing out of it or growing strong enough to bear it more easily, we must know that Christ is focused on saving us. We are often greatly tempted to doubt in times of immense pain. We doubt ourselves and our righteousness. We doubt that our God and our Savior are really paying much attention to us. Some wonder if there even is a God, and others feel that He has turned His back to them. These are the times of chastening, of tutelage, of testing, of preparation of our souls for a future harvest.

If you are not going to trust a loving Father and a Savior who died to save you, who *are* you going to trust in a world full of difficulties?

---

22 Philip. 4:7.
23 "'From Whom All Blessings Flow,'" *Ensign*, May 1997, 12.

Do you think you can trust in yourself alone? Are you powerful enough to overcome all things? Do you always know the right answer?

I know Latter-day Saints who have experienced enormous trials and, as a result, have lost trust in Heavenly Father and Jesus Christ. These friends have allowed their great pain to swell into a consuming anger. They have then ironically directed that anger toward the only Beings who can relieve their pain. There is no solace in such anger nor is there any ability to keep adversity at bay by keeping God away. By responding angrily toward a loving Savior, the original tragedy is only compounded.

You may have had terrible experiences come into your life, experiences for which you bear no blame. Such life events may have scarred you deeply and damaged your ability to trust anyone or anything. In some ways, the pain of the innocent can exceed the pain of the guilty in this life. To you I would ask a simple question. Do you want to continue living in your world of pain? If you do not, I ask another question. Do you know how to move out of your world of pain?

Jesus Christ is the God of broken people, the God of the hopeless, the God of the violated innocent, the God of ruined lives, the God of those who weep without ceasing. He is also and always will be the God of fresh starts, the God of new lives, the God of inner peace. His greatest ministry is where there is the greatest pain. There is no place so dark that He will not enter and bring a gentle and warming light.

"Come unto me, all ye that labour and are heavy laden, and I will give you rest."[24]

PROFOUND TRUST

Elder Richard G. Scott said, "This life is an experience in profound trust—trust in Jesus Christ, trust in His teachings, trust in our capacity as led by the Holy Spirit to obey those teachings for happiness now and for a purposeful, supremely happy eternal existence. To trust means to obey willingly without knowing the end from the beginning (see Proverbs 3:5–7). To produce fruit, your trust in the Lord must be more powerful and enduring than your confidence in your own personal feelings and experience."[25]

24   Matt. 11:28.
25   "Trust in the Lord," *Ensign*, Nov. 1995, 17.

Whose wounds and scars does Christ carry on His body? Whose pains did He endure? They are *our* wounds, *our* scars, *our* pains. We cannot tell Him anything about our suffering that He does not already know in the deepest part of His soul.

Whether we are wounded by terrible trials or scarred by vile sins, Christ takes our wounds and makes them His. He lifts them off us if we will allow Him to do so and enables us to heal and find peace. If we can learn and never forget this fundamental and most important truth, if we can get it into the deepest parts of our soul, we can enjoy the excellency of the knowledge of Jesus Christ. We will truly know Him and the power of His redemption through the intimate fellowship that we gain through His and our shared sufferings.

> *Oh, that each in the day*
> *Of His coming may say,*
> *"I have fought my way thru;*
> *I have finished the work*
> *Thou didst give me to do."*
> *Oh, that each from his Lord*
> *May receive the glad word:*
> *"Well and faithfully done;*
> *Enter into my joy and sit down on my throne;*
> *Enter into my joy and sit down on my throne."*

—"Come, Let Us Anew," *Hymns,* no. 217

"ARE WE NOT ALL BEGGARS?"— GOOD TIMES AND THE ATONEMENT

*Ye do not remember the Lord your God in the
things with which he hath blessed you, but ye do always
remember your riches, not to thank the Lord your God for them;
yea, your hearts are not drawn out unto the Lord, but they
do swell with great pride, unto boasting, and unto great
swelling, envyings, strifes, malice, persecutions,
and murders, and all manner of iniquities.*

—Helaman 13:22

*Take courage, brethren. . . . Plow your
land, and sow wheat, plant your potatoes. . . . It is
our duty to preach the gospel, gather Israel, pay our tithing
and build temples. The worst fear I have about this people is that
they will get rich in this country, forget God and his people,
wax fat, and kick themselves out of the Church and go
to hell. This people will stand mobbing, robbing,
poverty and all manner of persecution and be
true. But my greatest fear is that they
cannot stand wealth.*

—President Brigham Young, quoted in Harold B. Lee, *Decisions
for Successful Living* (Salt Lake City: Deseret Book, 1973), 212

WHY is there a need to discuss the Atonement in connection with
good times in our lives? Aren't peace, happiness, success, and

prosperity what we spend so much time and effort striving to achieve? When all is well, what special needs do we have?

An old story tells of a roofer who was working high up on a tall house, repairing storm damage. The roof was steep, and the roofer knew that he must be very careful to avoid a misstep that would cause him to lose his footing and slide off the roof and onto the ground.

Toward the end of a long day of work, just for a moment, he was inattentive to his safety. A foot slipped, and he fell, sliding downward on the slippery roof.

As he slid, the roofer prayed fervently. "Lord, please help me, or I will be badly hurt!"

Nothing happened. The roofer's speed increased as he tumbled down the roof toward its edge.

"Heavenly Father, I need help right now. Don't let me fall!" Again, there was no response.

The roofer knew he was nearing the edge of the roof and that when he fell off, he would be seriously injured or killed. In desperation he cried, "Father, please save me; please help me!"

At that moment, his heavy work belt snagged on a nail and his downward slide was stopped. As he lay at the edge of the roof, the roofer caught his breath and said, "Don't bother about my prayer, Lord. I don't need any help now."

In the first year of the reign of Zedekiah, the king of Judah, the children of Israel turned away from the commandments of the Lord. "In that same year there came many prophets, prophesying unto the people that they must repent, or the great city Jerusalem must be destroyed. . . . and the inhabitants thereof; many should perish by the sword, and many should be carried away captive into Babylon."[1]

When the citizens of Jerusalem failed to heed these warnings, Nebuchadnezzar and the armies of Babylon marched into the city, destroyed Solomon's temple, and carried the children of Israel into captivity. While in captivity, the Jews came under great pressure to give up their odd religion, assimilate, and become like the Babylonians. Although some succumbed to that pressure, others made a promise as they prayed, "If I forget thee, O Jerusalem, let my right

---

1   1 Ne. 1:4, 13.

hand forget her cunning. If I do not remember thee, let my tongue cleave to the roof of my mouth; if I prefer not Jerusalem above my chief joy."[2]

In their times of trial, these chosen people vowed that they would always remember their true spiritual home and that they would not forget their temple and their God. Somehow they would return to the place they belonged, the promised land. After many years, a great miracle occurred. The armies of Persia conquered Babylon, and King Cyrus freed the Jews.

The exiles returned to Jerusalem and rebuilt their temple. At first, they remembered their captivity and increased in faith and diligence. As time passed, however, the memories of their captivity and the miracles that freed them faded. They forgot their Lord, failed to heed His prophets, and lapsed first into neglect and then apostasy.

When the Messiah came to Jerusalem, most of its inhabitants had lost so much of their spiritual vision that they did not recognize Him. They thought they had remembered Jerusalem and its temple and their religion, but they had forgotten the spirit of their Babylonian prayer and had become a mere caricature of the great and faithful tribes of ancient Israel. They had forgotten the true purpose of the Mosaic law and were blind to its fulfillment.

Nephi foretold the fate of these forgetful Jews, "And as for those who are at Jerusalem, saith the prophet, they shall be scourged by all people, because they crucify the God of Israel, and turn their hearts aside, rejecting signs and wonders, and the power and glory of the God of Israel. And because they turn their hearts aside, saith the prophet, and have despised the Holy One of Israel, they shall wander in the flesh, and perish, and become a hiss and a byword, and be hated among all nations."[3]

About thirty-five years following the Savior's crucifixion, the debased temple at Jerusalem was permanently destroyed, and the children of Israel were scattered to the four corners of the earth. Most forgot who they were and vanished into the gentile world. The small fragment who remembered were condemned to a state of almost helpless victimhood, hated of all nations, for nearly two thousand years.

---

2 Psa. 137:5–6.

3 1 Ne.19:13–14.

As I have written elsewhere in this book, tribulation in all its forms severely tries our faith, but we are not generally inclined to forget our Heavenly Father at such times. Some Saints may lose their grasp on the gospel in the face of terrible difficulties, but even they do not *begin* by forgetting God. Just like the roofer, our *first* reaction to almost any trial is to pray for relief, and it is easy to remember to continually plead for help as long as we're sliding toward certain destruction.

In the absence of imminent danger, however, we are also prone to respond like the roofer and become negligent of our Savior and blind to the blessings He bestows upon us. Only if another misstep sends us hurtling toward disaster do we remember to turn our attention back to Him.

Just as Nephi foretold the perilous condition of many of the inhabitants of Jerusalem when they "turn[ed] their hearts aside"[4] and rejected the Savior, he also prophesied of one of the greatest dangers of our day, "And others will he pacify, and lull them away into carnal security, that they will say: All is well in Zion; yea, Zion prospereth, all is well—and thus the devil cheateth their souls, and leadeth them away carefully down to hell."[5]

We spend an enormous amount of time and effort to make our mortal lives successful and often face great opposition and difficulty as we strive to do so. Unconsciously, we sometimes conclude that if we can only reach a place that we have defined as success, our own personal Jerusalem (viewed from Babylon), that our struggles will be over and our life will become easy.

It is common for our definition of success to include accomplishments or possessions recognized by the world. When the degree is finished, when we can buy a house, when we secure a job that pays a good salary, when the children are all married in the temple, when we have accumulated so many dollars in savings and investments, when we are able to retire, everything will be fine, our troubles and trials will be over.

If we feel that our testing is done, that everything has become easy, that there are no more spiritual hills to climb, I think we must

---

4   1 Ne. 19:14.

5   2 Ne. 28:21.

look for the effects of the anesthetic that Satan seems to apply to those he is quietly and without fanfare carefully dragging down to hell.

FOR WHERE YOUR TREASURE IS

Elder Neal A. Maxwell said, "I don't think God's too interested in real estate. He owns it all anyway. He does seem to be incredibly interested in what happens to us individually and will place us in those circumstances where we have the most opportune chances to grow and to carry out our purposes."[6]

If God is not too interested in real estate, what does that tell us about devoting all of our best thoughts and best hours to real estate or some other business that has little significance, if any, while we live upon this earth? Further, what does it tell us about the consequences if we are very successful in real estate or some other business but not successful in matters that God *is* interested in?

The Lord is very interested in our hearts. "For where your treasure is, there will your heart be also."[7]

The scriptures contain warning after warning concerning the dangers of riches, emphasizing their power to attract the hearts of men and thereby destroy their souls:

- "These men have set up their idols in their heart."[8]
- "Behold ye, the people of this great city, and hearken unto my words; yea, hearken unto the words which the Lord saith; for behold, he saith that *ye are cursed because of your riches, and also are your riches cursed because ye have set your hearts upon them, and have not hearkened unto the words of him who gave them unto you.*"[9]
- "Behold, O my God, their costly apparel, and their ringlets, and their bracelets, and their ornaments of gold, and all their

---

6   "But for a Small Moment," fireside address given at Brigham Young University on 1 Sept. 1974.

7   Matt. 6:21; see also Luke 12:34; 3 Ne. 13:21.

8   Ezek. 14:3.

9   Hel. 13:21; emphasis added.

precious things which they are ornamented with; and behold, *their hearts are set upon them,* and yet they cry unto thee and say—We thank thee, O God, for we are a chosen people unto thee, while others shall perish."[10]

- "If riches increase, set not your heart upon them."[11]
- "Why do ye set your hearts upon riches?"[12]

In contrast to the warnings about misplacing the priorities of our hearts, the continuing affirmative "heart" commandment of the Lord is clear: "Now set your heart and your soul to seek the Lord your God."[13]

The hearts of the people are key to whether they are able to experience wealth and righteousness at the same time. Many, perhaps even most, are not able to do so, and thus we see a multitude of prophetic warnings of danger here.

The first chapter of Alma records that after King Mosiah died and the reign of the judges had begun, there was a great division among the Nephites. On the one hand, some followed the false doctrines and priestcrafts of Nehor and became prideful. Their hearts were set upon their riches, and they committed a wide variety of serious sins: "Those who did not belong to their church did indulge themselves in sorceries, and in idolatry or idleness, and in babblings, and in envyings and strife; wearing costly apparel; *being lifted up in the pride of their own eyes*; persecuting, lying, thieving, robbing, committing whoredoms, and murdering, and all manner of wickedness."[14]

During this period, the wicked continually oppressed and persecuted the righteous members of the Church. Despite such treatment, the followers of Christ prospered greatly, even more than their oppressors did. The attitude with which the righteous regarded their riches differed substantially from that of their wicked brethren:

---

10   Alma 31:28; emphasis added.
11   Psa. 62:10.
12   Mosiah 12:29.
13   1 Chron. 22:19.
14   Alma 1:32; emphasis added.

And they did impart of their substance, every man according to that which he had, to the poor, and the needy, and the sick, and the afflicted; and they did not wear costly apparel, yet they were neat and comely. . . .

And now, *because of the steadiness of the church they began to be exceedingly rich,* having abundance of all things whatsoever they stood in need—an abundance of flocks and herds, and fatlings of every kind, and also abundance of grain, and of gold, and of silver, and of precious things, and abundance of silk and fine-twined linen, and all manner of good homely cloth.

And thus, in their prosperous circumstances, they did not send away any who were naked, or that were hungry, or that were athirst, or that were sick, or that had not been nourished; and *they did not set their hearts upon riches*; therefore they were liberal to all, both old and young, both bond and free, both male and female, whether out of the church or in the church, having no respect to persons as to those who stood in need.[15]

The same people at the same time and same place obtained riches and responded in two radically different ways. One group focused their hearts upon the riches of the world. The other group had worldly riches but focused their hearts on the treasure that only the Savior can give. The heart is the key, the indicator of where our true riches are, and we cannot pretend that our hearts are wholly given to the Lord when they are not. Fortunately, the Atonement of Christ has the power to change our hearts if we will allow it to do so.

"Seek not for riches but for wisdom, and behold, the mysteries of God shall be unfolded unto you, and then shall you be made rich. Behold, he that hath eternal life is rich."[16]

---

15   Alma 1:27, 29–30; emphasis added.

16   D&C 6:7.

Who Shall Ascend into the Hill of the Lord?

We live in a world in which the accumulation of material wealth and all its accoutrements is the passion of many. The wealthy celebrate themselves and are celebrated by others. As Brother Brigham foresaw, some members of the Church have become materially wealthy, and of those, a portion have kicked themselves out of the Church and the kingdom of God in consequence.

Some people minimize the danger that material wealth can present. "I wish that I had that problem," they may say. "My troubles are just the opposite." These people might be shocked to learn that when they pray for the Lord's help in avoiding temptation, part of His response to that prayer might be to insulate them from too much worldly success.

The dangers of worldly success and accompanying pride should not be minimized. These temptations are real and ongoing. Succumbing to them will deprive a person of the eternal rewards of virtue and faith just as surely as will murder, theft, or violating the law of chastity.

Several years ago, I attended a business meeting with a man who worked in a small department of a large financial services company. This department was devoted to providing a wide range of services to extremely wealthy people. As I recall, only clients with one hundred million dollars or more in assets would qualify for these services.

Following our business discussion, I spoke to this man about his work. I asked what types of problems he helped his wealthy clients solve. I was expecting an answer involving investments, taxes, or financial planning, so his response surprised me, "The thing that worries these people more than anything else is that their money will ruin their children's lives. They have seen that happen in other wealthy families and want to know what they can do to avoid it in their own."

To help address this problem, this man, who was a member of the Church, met with his clients to teach them about the importance of holding regular family gatherings. During these family meetings, he encouraged the parents to discuss fundamental values that had nothing to do with money. He counseled them to talk to their children about the importance of using the family's wealth responsibly, including generously assisting others who had less. This wealth manager freely admitted that he drew upon many of the principles underlying the Church's family home evening program in his work.

It was ironic that these wealthy people paid what were undoubtedly large service fees to learn soul-saving principles that the poorest LDS family can understand without charge. The biggest concerns they brought to their wealth managers had to do with their families, not their worldly possessions.

The Psalmist asks and answers the most important question of our material lives, "Who shall ascend into the hill of the Lord? or who shall stand in his holy place? He that hath clean hands, and a pure heart; who hath not lifted up his soul unto vanity, nor sworn deceitfully."[17] Anything whatsoever that interferes with the purity of our hearts, our absolute focus upon our Lord and Savior, Jesus Christ, will kick us out of the kingdom unless we repent and put it in its proper place.

SUFFICIENTLY HUMBLE

How can we avoid the trap of forgetting God during the good times of our lives? Alma the Younger provides a spiritual checklist for us, one that requires us to always apply the Atonement.

When Alma presented his great Atonement sermon in Zarahemla recorded in Alma 5, he was dealing with a prideful people who were in the process of kicking themselves out of the kingdom. He began his teaching by reminding his audience of the captivity of their fathers. He recounted how Alma the Elder taught their fathers the gospel and how the Lord delivered them from captivity. He then began to describe how the people of Zarahemla could be released from the bondage of pride that trapped them.

In Alma 5:14–16, Alma asked these people a series of important questions. We also need to bring these questions to our minds on a regular basis, particularly when our lives are going well. I have changed the form of Alma's questions so we can ask them of ourselves:

---

17   Psa. 24:3–4.

- Have I spiritually been born of God?
- Have I received His image in my countenance?
- Have I experienced a mighty change in my heart?
- Do I exercise faith in the redemption of Him who created me?
- Do I look forward with an eye of faith, and view my mortal body raised in immortality and my corruption raised in incorruption, to stand before God to be judged according to the deeds which I have done in my mortal body?
- Can I imagine to myself that I hear the voice of the Lord, saying unto me, in that day: Come unto me ye blessed, for behold, your works have been the works of righteousness upon the face of the earth?

The Spirit had already revealed to Alma the answers to those questions for many of the people of Zarahemla, and they were not good answers. Because the people need additional help, Alma asks another series of more pointed questions in verses 17–24. Again, I have changed the form of these questions:

- Do I imagine to myself that I can lie to the Lord in that day [the day of my judgment], and say—Lord, my works have been righteous works upon the face of the earth—and that He will save me?
- Can I imagine myself brought before the tribunal of God with my soul filled with guilt and remorse, having a remembrance of all my guilt, a perfect remembrance of all my wickedness, a remembrance that I have set at defiance the commandments of God?
- Can I look up to God at that day with a pure heart and clean hands?
- Can I look up, having the image of God engraven upon my countenance?
- Can I think of being saved when I have yielded myself to become subject to the devil?
- How will I feel if I stand before the bar of God, having my garments stained with blood and all manner of filthiness?

- What will these things testify against me? Will they not testify that I am guilty of all manner of wickedness?
- Do I suppose that I can have a place to sit down in the kingdom of God, with Abraham, with Isaac, and with Jacob, and also all the holy prophets, whose garments are cleansed and are spotless, pure, and white?

After this series of questions, at least some of the people in Zarahemla are pricked in their consciences. They certainly understand that, due to their behavior and neglect, they carry the filthiness of the world upon them.

What are they to do? Where is the path that will lead them away from their sins and take them back to a place where they can feel confident to stand before the Lord and be judged?

Alma asks yet another series of questions in verses 27–30. These questions represent our daily work as Saints, a checklist for regular repentance, the way we measure how we are doing when we wake up in the morning and when we go to bed at night. These questions highlight some of the biggest challenges that can come to us when we are in the midst of prosperity and good times.

If I were called to die *today*, how would I answer these questions?

- Am I sufficiently humble?
- Are my garments cleansed by the blood of Christ?
- Am I stripped of pride?
- Am I stripped of envy?
- Do I mock others?
- Do I persecute others?

The proper answer to all of these questions requires the ongoing daily application of both the cleansing power and the enabling and strengthening power of the Atonement.

STRIPPED OF PRIDE

In his first general conference after becoming president and prophet, Ezra Taft Benson gave an address that had a great impact on the Church. He said:

In the scriptures there is no such thing as righteous pride. It is always considered as a sin. We are not speaking of a wholesome view of self-worth, which is best established by a close relationship with God. But *we are speaking of pride as the universal sin,* as someone has described it.

Mormon writes that "the pride of this nation, or the people of the Nephites, hath proven their destruction" (Moroni 8:27). The Lord says in the Doctrine and Covenants, "Beware of pride, lest ye become as the Nephites of old" (38:39).

Essentially, pride is a "my will" rather than "thy will" approach to life. The opposite of pride is humbleness, meekness, submissiveness (Alma 13:28) or teachableness. . . .

Pride does not look up to God and care about what is right. It looks sideways to man and argues who is right. Pride is manifest in the spirit of contention.

Was it not through pride that the devil became the devil? Christ wanted to serve. The devil wanted to rule. Christ wanted to bring men to where He was. The devil wanted to be above men.

Christ removed self as the force in His perfect life. It was not *my* will, but *thine* be done.

Pride is characterized by "What do I want out of life?" rather than by "What would God have me do with my life?" It is self-will as opposed to God's will. It is the fear of man over the fear of God.[18]

Pride is one of the greatest threats to our spiritual welfare when our lives are going well. It is ever a temptation to compare our circumstances to those around us who are experiencing trials and conclude that our life's external successes are a reflection of our internal virtue. We often think, *If those people who are having problems would simply live as well as I do, their lives would be successful.*

---

18   "Cleansing the Inner Vessel," 6–7; emphasis added.

Pride will destroy us spiritually as surely as any other sin. Pride is particularly ugly if it is our response when the Lord has provided us with blessings of wealth, talent, security, or peace. Pride will certainly end that security and peace sooner or later. When pride rules our thoughts and emotions, we are undeniably an enemy to God and man alike. Pride is why the devil became the devil.

President Henry B. Eyring has also warned of the spiritual dangers that can lie in the midst of worldly success and the pride that sometimes accompanies it. Sometimes we envision the fall of the proud as a great cataclysm, a life that collapses in ruins, but Satan is far too clever to utilize this tactic, particularly early in his seduction of the egotistical. President Eyring has said that far more frequently, the descent is gradual, a dimming of the light so imperceptible to the person in decline that their eyes adjust to the gathering darkness and nothing significant seems to have changed.

At first, he misses a church meeting here or there, but nothing bad seems to happen. The adversary's target still feels fine, and it seems like a relief to be able to rest instead of getting up, getting dressed, and going to a meeting that seems unrewarding. Absences from church become more frequent, tithing payments are missed, but worldly success continues and may even increase. Somehow, the prideful man or woman expects that there would be a clear warning from God, some disaster that would come into their lives if their path were really a dangerous one.

A spiritual paralysis slowly spreads. Friends may try to intervene, the bishop may call, but all this seems silly to the prideful man or woman. "I'm still on the team," they tell themselves. "I'm just resting on the bench for a few innings. I'll get back in the game one of these days. I deserve a break after so many years of being a conforming little Mormon."

New friends who do not live LDS standards become increasingly attractive. They are so much more sophisticated than the parochial Saints scurrying here and there trying to be perfect, never taking the opportunity so smell the roses and enjoy the "good life." The conversation is far more intelligent and entertaining at the country club than it is in Elders Quorum or Relief Society.

Pride continues to grow, crowding out faith, obedience, charity, and all other fruits of humility. Testimony fades with disuse, and the still small voice becomes indiscernible. Satan's invitations feel so good and seem so harmless and easy. The flaxen cord is imperceptible at first, but it never leaves, and the longer it is present, the easier it is for the adversary to guide the proud away from light and freedom.[19] "He leadeth them by the neck with a flaxen cord, until he bindeth them with his strong cords forever."[20]

When we are experiencing our Liberty Jails, it's less difficult to control pride, but when those experiences are absent, we must be careful to fill the void left by the absence of tribulation with something both virtuous and humble. Driving a fancy pickup truck across Wyoming doesn't provide the same degree of spiritual protection that pulling a handcart along the same route does.

Succor Those That Stand in Need of Your Succor

Paul described the potential fruits of tribulation when he says, "We glory in tribulations also: knowing that tribulation worketh patience; And patience, experience; and experience, hope."[21] This statement raises a question. If our life is free from tribulation, how will we gain real patience? Or experience or hope? These are, of course, important spiritual characteristics, and I believe that we must constantly work on the development of such attributes. Can we imagine a faithful servant of Christ who is not patient? Patience is a primary virtue that travels in convoy with other fundamental Christian virtues. "Be patient; be sober; be temperate; have patience, faith, hope and charity."[22] Is it possible for a person to be charitable without patience?

As Paul describes it, tribulation can be the trigger that commences the construction of vitally important spiritual traits in our lives.

I have previously discussed the important questions Alma asks in Alma 5, spiritual questions that comprise a personal audit list that is of special significance during good times. An even more fundamental

---

19   "A Life Founded in Light and Truth," devotional address given at Brigham Young University on 15 Aug. 2000.

20   2 Ne. 26:22.

21   Rom. 5:3–4.

22   D&C 6:19.

answer to the question, "How do I continue spiritual growth when life is easy and tribulation absent?" is found in the Atonement.

King Benjamin taught that answer well. After he preached his great Atonement sermon, convincing his people of their need for a Savior and the necessity of repentance from their sins, an amazing thing happened.

> And they [the Nephites listening to King Benjamin] all cried aloud with one voice, saying: O have mercy, and apply the atoning blood of Christ that we may receive forgiveness of our sins, and our hearts may be purified; for we believe in Jesus Christ, the Son of God. . . .
>
> And it came to pass that after they had spoken these words the Spirit of the Lord came upon them, and they were filled with joy, having received a remission of their sins, and having peace of conscience, because of the exceeding faith which they had in Jesus Christ who should come.[23]

At this point, the spiritual condition of the Nephites was excellent, and it sounds as if they were as perfect and clean as they could be. They had learned of the Atonement, applied it in their lives, and been forgiven of their sins. Their hearts had been changed in a profound and wonderful way. They were spiritually successful and at peace.

Wise King Benjamin knew that this supernal moment would pass, however, so he taught them what they must do to retain this wonderful condition. What would they do tomorrow and the next day and all the other days of their lives to consolidate and extend the spiritual gains that they had just accomplished through the atoning blood of Christ? Following are King Benjamin's prophetic answers:

> Ye yourselves will succor those that stand in need of your succor; ye will administer of your substance unto him that standeth in need; and ye will not suffer

---

23   Mosiah 4:2–3.

that the beggar putteth up his petition to you in vain, and turn him out to perish. . . .

For behold, are we not all beggars? Do we not all depend upon the same Being, even God, for all the substance which we have, for both food and raiment, and for gold, and for silver, and for all the riches which we have of every kind? . . .

And now, if God, who has created you, on whom you are dependent for your lives and for all that ye have and are, doth grant unto you whatsoever ye ask that is right, in faith, believing that ye shall receive, O then, how ye ought to impart of the substance that ye have one to another.[24]

King Benjamin interweaves two themes in these verses:

* You must help others—Succor those who stand in need of your succor.
* As you provide such assistance with the right heart, you will continue to be humble and stripped of pride—Are we not all beggars? You and the beggar living in an alley are each constantly dependent upon God for your life and all that you have and are.

Serving others because we love Christ will help us maintain and develop the vital characteristics of patience, humility, and charity. Especially when we are doing well, when tribulation is not our primary instructor, we must do good for others.

Elder Maxwell has written, "Those who worry if they currently seem to be untested should not feel guilty or anxious, nor should they pray for trials. First of all, the absence of major tribulation can, ironically, produce the trial of tranquility with its very grave risks of careless ease. Second, *the Lord does require a few intact individuals and families to help others manage their trials and tribulations,* even though these roles often rotate. . . . Third, life is not over yet, and there can

---

24   Mosiah 4:16, 19, 21.

be, as we have all seen, a tremendous compression of trials. Finally, the absence of . . . trials . . . arising out of our own sins and mistakes, is obviously never to be regretted."[25]

Retaining a Remission of Your Sins

As he instructed the repentant Nephites on how to build upon their spiritual success, King Benjamin made a direct connection between the Atonement and giving our abundance to others, "And now, for the sake of these things which I have spoken unto you—that is, *for the sake of retaining a remission of your sins from day to day*, that ye may walk guiltless before God—I would that ye should impart of your substance to the poor, every man according to that which he hath, such as feeding the hungry, clothing the naked, visiting the sick and administering to their relief, both spiritually and temporally, according to their wants."[26]

Retaining the remission of our sins that we receive from our Savior, the vertical aspect of the Atonement, includes service to others, the horizontal aspect of the Atonement. The Savior has provided an infinite service to us and, if our hearts have been changed as we understand that service, He asks us, as His followers, to give to and help others. As we do so, we further change our hearts and become a little more like Christ.

One Sunday, after conducting interviews in the bishop's office on campus, I drove toward my student ward to deliver some Church manuals I had received earlier that week. As I traveled, I was thinking of the words of King Benjamin about the connection between retaining a remission of our sins and being beggars.

As the words, "Are we not all beggars? Do we not all depend upon that same Being, even God, for all the substance which we have?" passed through my mind, I saw a woman standing at the corner of my ward, right on the boundary. She appeared to be in her fifties and was poorly dressed. She was holding a piece of cardboard. On the cardboard, a single word was written, "Homeless."

I was stunned. The words of King Benjamin burned in my mind. Are we not all beggars? I am aware of good reasons why it may be

---

25   *All These Things*, 31–32; emphasis added.
26   Mosiah 4:26; emphasis added.

better to contribute to charities that help the homeless than it is to give money directly to the people, but this was not a coincidence. This woman was standing at the corner of my ward as I was thinking about beggars. She was a messenger from God for me.

I made a U-turn and stopped my car beside her.

I looked at the woman carefully. Her face was lined in the way people look when they have spent a lot of time outside. She had tried to comb her hair. There was some ground-in dirt on her face, but she looked calm, not crazy. A part of me wondered if she were even real. Another part of me wondered if she would say something to me, so clearly did I understand that she was a messenger from God.

I gave the woman money. She quietly said, "Thank you." Nothing more. After waiting for a moment, I drove on.

I thought about what had happened to me throughout the remainder of the day.

The woman received money from me—more than I have ever given anyone who was begging on the street but still a small amount for me, not anything that I would miss or that was difficult to give. What did I receive from that beggar? By responding to her request for assistance, I retained a remission of my sins. Which one of us received the most? Clearly, I did. She only received money that would be spent and gone in a few days. I received a chance to remain clean before my Heavenly Father for a while longer. I moved a tiny bit closer to eternal life.

There are beggars all around us. There is never a shortage nor will there ever be a shortage of those who need the succor we can give. Most beggars don't carry signs announcing their needs.

Some beggars live in large houses and may even have servants who minister to their physical needs. These beggars may be desperate for our help with spiritual or emotional hunger. They will probably never express their desperation, but Heavenly Father knows, and, if we listen, the Holy Ghost will direct us to them and tell us how to succor them.

Other beggars hide away in small rooms, trailers, garages, or basements in a part of town we seldom visit. We will have to actively search out these beggars and, perhaps, overcome their fear that we have come to harm them instead of help them. They may not know how to thank us, but Jesus will thank us for feeding His sheep.

We always have the ability to assist beggars. We may not have money to give, but James wrote that pure religion is to "visit the fatherless and widows in their affliction."[27] We can visit. We can telephone. We can write. We can go to the beggars and, like Lori, the artist who drew sketches in the nursing home, acknowledge each of them as a unique and wonderful child of God. We can take their hands in ours and remind the beggars that Jesus sacrificed Himself to save them because He loved them then and still loves them now.

If you ask your Heavenly Father, He will show you where to go and what to do to feed His sheep.

Your Troubles and Trials Are Through

Eliza R. Snow penned a tart warning against complacency in the opening words of a hymn: "Think not when you gather to Zion, Your troubles and trials are through."[28]

When we are in the midst of trials, we pray that they will end. When the Lord responds to our prayers and peace and calm enter our lives, we understandably feel that what we have prayed for has come—our trials have ended.

While the Lord certainly provides us with islands of tranquility from time to time (and we are most appreciative of them), if that tranquility goes on and on and it appears that tribulation is permanently banished from our lives, perhaps we need to examine our surroundings carefully. If we are not alert, the good times in our lives can become a spiritual soporific that lulls us into a committed engagement with whatever mortal successes accompany those good times. If they lead us to forget why we are here on this earth and what our mortal mission is, those good times will suit Satan's aim to divert us from our real purpose in this life.

As the time neared when Christ would be born in the land of Israel, the prophet Nephi, the son of Helaman, on the American continent, received a comprehensive education on the symptoms and dangers of pride as he watched the Nephites fall in love with the fruits of their prosperity:

---

27   James 1:27.
28   "Think Not, When You Gather to Zion," *Hymns* (1948 edition), no. 21.

And thus we can behold how false, and also the unsteadiness of the hearts of the children of men; yea, we can see that the Lord in his great infinite goodness doth bless and prosper those who put their trust in him.

Yea, and we may see at the very time when he doth prosper his people, yea, in the increase of their fields, their flocks and their herds, and in gold, and in silver, and in all manner of precious things of every kind and art; sparing their lives, and delivering them out of the hands of their enemies; softening the hearts of their enemies that they should not declare wars against them; yea, and in fine, doing all things for the welfare and happiness of his people; yea, *then is the time that they do harden their hearts, and do forget the Lord their God, and do trample under their feet the Holy One—yea, and this because of their ease, and their exceedingly great prosperity.*

And thus we see that except the Lord doth chasten his people with many afflictions, yea, except he doth visit them with death and with terror, and with famine and with all manner of pestilence, they will not remember him. . . .

Yea, how quick to be lifted up in pride; yea, how quick to boast, and do all manner of that which is iniquity; and how slow are they to remember the Lord their God, and to give ear unto his counsels, yea, how slow to walk in wisdom's paths![29]

Throughout our lives, whether the storms blow or the sun shines, our only hope, our only salvation, lies with Jesus Christ. We must continually focus and refocus our hearts and minds upon Him and doing whatever work He has for us. Service to others will help that focus. Humility will help that focus. Never forgetting that Christ is the source of all our blessings and that we receive those blessings through His grace is an essential character trait for the truly successful Christian.

---

29   Helaman 12:1–3, 5; emphasis added.

We may not know, we cannot tell,
What pains he had to bear,
But we believe it was for us
He hung and suffered there.

—"There Is a Green Hill Far Away," *Hymns,* no. 194

"ABIDE WITH ME"—PRAYER AND THE ATONEMENT

Search diligently, pray always, and be believing.

—D&C 90:24

How does knowing that Christ is my lifeline and my communication line to the Father affect my prayers?

Christ has died for me and has promised that He will intercede for me with the Father. My Savior has told me, "Listen to him who is the advocate with the Father, who is pleading your cause before him—Saying: Father, behold the sufferings and death of him who did no sin, in whom thou wast well pleased; behold the blood of thy Son which was shed, the blood of him whom thou gavest that thyself might be glorified; Wherefore, Father, spare these my brethren that believe on my name, that they may come unto me and have everlasting life."[1]

When I'm praying to my Heavenly Father, Christ is adding His mighty voice to my puny one, pointing out His sacrifice for me as He speaks with a greater wisdom and power than I ever possibly could. Because God's ways are not man's ways, however, and Christ's desire first and foremost is that I return to be with my Father, the answers to my prayers may not be what I expect them to be.

After I was called to be bishop of the BYU singles ward but before I was sustained, I had a personal concern. I have always had difficulty remembering the names of new people I meet. I can easily remember faces, but names often elude me. I have lived in a variety of places, but leadership callings typically have come after I have had a period of

---

1   D&C 45:3–5.

time during which I could learn and remember names of those people I've been working with.

Beginning with my first Sunday on campus, I would be meeting about one hundred and fifty men and women in my new ward all at once. Each semester would bring more new members into the ward. I was called as a representative of the Lord. He knew their names, and I should, as well. It had never occurred to me before that I should pray about this particular shortcoming, but I did so, asking for a gift of the Spirit to remember names while I was bishop.

I made it through my first Sunday without anyone expecting me to remember any names. After all, I was a brand-new bishop. I received a ward directory with photographs and studied it carefully on Sunday evening, but nothing seemed to stick. On Monday, we held a combined family home evening picnic for all members of the ward, and I tried to meet as many students as possible, discovering something about each of them in the process. I was definitely enjoying the experience of becoming acquainted with these amazing people, but I still worried that I would fail to recall their names from memory when the need arose. I did feel a spiritual impression of each person, however, and began to understand how important my ward members were to the Lord and how much He loved these daughters and sons.

One of our activities that evening was a coed game of ultimate Frisbee. As I watched the game, I began to think, "John just passed to Chelise, and she threw the Frisbee to Matt," almost like a play-by-play broadcaster. As the Frisbee flew from player to player, the name of each person quickly entered my mind. I realized that my prayer was being answered. Their names were being provided to me in part because the Lord had revealed their spirits to me. I asked for names, and the Lord showed me spirits instead. Each name that came into my mind was accompanied by insights into who this person really was.

I had many similar experiences as I served as the bishop for an incredible group of people. Often, I received a quick spiritual message about a person, delivered faster than I could think. Of course, I prayed for specific members of my ward by name and received answers to my prayers. However, sometimes my rapid and vivid spiritual impressions did not seem to be answers to prayers that I had uttered. Over time, I realized that they were answers to prayers that I *should* have offered. *Heavenly Father wanted me to know more than I was asking to know.*

FROM THE CAMPUS TO THE WORLD

It took me some time to apply these bishop's experiences to my own personal prayers. At one point, I was praying about a professional decision. This was a very important decision, one without a good answer that I could not discover by thought and reason. I reviewed the problem in my mind over and over but was unable to come to any decision that made sense to me. There were not several possible answers from which to choose; there was no answer.

I repeatedly prayed about what I should do, asking the same questions again and again. This was a critical issue, and I needed, really needed, clear direction. Part of each prayer was a request that Heavenly Father would answer my prayer in a definite and unambiguous way. I didn't want to make a mistake about this. A wrong choice could have very serious consequences for myself and my family.

No answer came.

One night, after a long evening of ward interviews, I was thinking about the contrast between my experiences as a bishop and my professional problem. In my Church role, divine guidance often came so effortlessly. I could move from one difficult situation to another with the members of my ward and always feel the Spirit. I could clearly discern their problems. I could quickly receive revelation for struggling men and women and give counsel that was far wiser than my mortal mind could have produced. Without doubt or hesitation, I could reassure my ward members that God was mindful of their needs, that He heard their prayers, that they had a Savior, and that through His Atonement, He would deliver them from their trials or help them with their decisions. I could promise them that answers would come. The Spirit was present and confirmed to my ward members and me that what I said was true.

Why did the divine inspiration that worked so well for Bishop Vandagriff not seem to be helping Brother Vandagriff?

At first I thought that it was because the members of my ward were such wonderful and committed sons and daughters of God with so many important future missions that He would, of course, tell me what to say and do in order to quickly help them. The amazing spiritual experiences I was sharing were not about the bishop but rather about the member.

This was true, undoubtedly true, but did it really explain why Brother Vandagriff was having so much difficulty getting his answer?

Maybe it was because I was less valiant or had less spiritual potential. As I contemplated this possibility, Heavenly Father was kind enough to reassure me that His love did not vary with the recipient. Each of His children receives all of His infinite love. He sent His Firstborn Son to save every spirit child, regardless of their circumstances in this life. God heard every prayer, including mine.

Why was there a difference then? Why could I receive revelation so quickly as bishop but have no detailed and direct answer elsewhere?

Then I understood. When I received a quick flash of guidance in the bishop's office, I acted on it immediately and confidently, even when I was dealing with a ward member in very serious trouble. I paid close attention to the whisperings of the Holy Ghost under those circumstances.

In my personal life, I was attempting to demand more of God. "This is an important decision for me," I was thinking, "so I need to have more than a quick flash of guidance. I must have my answer spelled out in detail and confirmed with spiritual power that will resonate from the top of my head to the soles of my feet."

Without fully realizing it, I was presuming to tell God how to do His job when He answered my personal prayers. Instead of taking whatever He provided me and being grateful for it, like I did in the bishop's office, I was demanding that He give me exactly the answer I wanted at that time in my personal life. I was asking the Holy Ghost to speak with a loud voice to me on this topic. No wonder I "wasn't getting any answer." I was looking for a rocket in the sky rather than a candle in the window.

How many times had I done this before with other problems?

I prayed for forgiveness more than once. I prayed for understanding of what I had done in the past and how I needed to change. I discovered that it was far easier to repent than to live with the consequences of my error—not opening my heart to His answers.

Shortly thereafter, a quick impression came into my mind about my business problem. This was an unconventional idea, something that had never occurred to me. Almost by reflex, I asked myself, "Is this real? What if it doesn't work?" Then, I had another quick impression that can be summarized in two words, "Pay attention!" I could imagine the Holy Ghost shaking His head, thinking, "When will this guy ever learn?"

I worked to develop the idea. The work was easy. Everything I needed to follow up on my impression quickly fell into place. Then I moved forward. The solution worked right away.

Here again, the great wisdom of King Benjamin was confirmed. I hadn't been relying on the Atonement. I was a natural man when I was dealing with what I thought was a worldly matter, and that put me in opposition to God. I wasn't in active rebellion against God, but I was caught up in worldly concerns, stumbling around as if I didn't understand His gospel and what He wanted me to be. I needed to put off the natural man and become a saint through the Atonement, becoming submissive, meek, and humble—not just on Sunday or in my Church calling but every day and in every aspect of my life.[2]

"Inasmuch as you strip yourselves from jealousies and fears, and humble yourselves before me, for ye are not sufficiently humble, the veil shall be rent and you shall see me and know that I am—*not with the carnal neither natural mind, but with the spiritual*."[3]

I had forgotten that all things are spiritual with God. I was carnally minded, not in the sense of thinking of bodily lusts but in the sense that my mind was focused on worldly solutions to worldly problems instead of upon the Spirit. In my search for answers, I was foolishly limiting the Spirit to working with what I thought were spiritual matters instead of allowing Him to influence and direct all parts of my life.

"Yea, behold, I will tell you in your mind and in your heart, by the Holy Ghost, which shall come upon you and which shall dwell in your heart. Now, behold, *this is the spirit of revelation*; behold, this is the spirit by which Moses brought the children of Israel through the Red Sea on dry ground. Therefore *this is thy gift; apply unto it*,

---

2   See Mosiah 3:19.

3   D&C 67:10; emphasis added.

and blessed art thou, for it shall deliver you out of the hands of your enemies, when, if it were not so, they would slay you and bring your soul to destruction. Oh, remember these words, and keep my commandments. *Remember, this is your gift.*"[4]

My mind and heart had to be welded together. Did not Christ show the way? Gethsemane required all of His mighty mind and every part of His loving heart. If I am to be a faithful follower of His, I also have to offer all that I am, all of my mind, and all of my heart. That's the way the Atonement works. I do all that I can do, and then my Savior and His Atonement bridge the vast distance between my best efforts and my Father's celestial standard. It will work; it absolutely will work, but only if I give everything and hold back nothing, only if I place myself entirely in the Lord's hands.

Elder Bruce C. Hafen has described the unbalanced bargain of the Atonement. "So we must willingly give everything, because God Himself can't make us grow against our will and without our full participation. *Yet even when we utterly spend ourselves, we lack the power to create the perfection only God can complete. Our* all *by itself is still only* almost *enough—until it is finished by the* all *of Him who is the 'finisher of our faith.'* At that point, our imperfect but consecrated *almost* is enough."[5]

MAHONRI AND OLIVER

We have a lesson on how to draw on heaven's power in the stories of two good men who each asked for help: Mahonri Moriancumer (the brother of Jared) and Oliver Cowdery.

Mahonri was "a man highly favored of the Lord,"[6] and his prayers were powerful, leading his people away from the Tower of Babel when the languages were confounded. Then the Lord challenged the Jaredite's faith and told them to travel to the unknown. "And it came to pass that the Lord commanded them that they should go forth into the wilderness, yea, *into that quarter where there never had man been.*"[7]

---

4   D&C 8:2–5; emphasis added.

5   "The Atonement: All for All," *Liahona*, May 2004, 98–99; emphasis added.

6   Ether 1:34.

7   Ether 2:5; emphasis added.

Like the children of Israel coming out of Egypt, the Jaredites found that "the Lord did go before them, and did talk with them as he stood in a cloud, and gave directions whither they should travel."[8]

They traveled through the uncharted desert and came to the edge of a great sea where they camped for four years. This place must have been a great relief after hundreds of miles of travel. At last, they could stop and rest. Times were good. Food and water were plentiful. Many Jaredites had undoubtedly prayed for an end to the desert and believed the seaside was the answer to their prayers.

At some time during this period on the beach, the brother of Jared, among the most faithful followers of Christ in any age, made a significant error. He stopped praying. After all the miracles, protection, and blessings, and after speaking with the Lord in a cloud, Mahonri stopped praying, and the Lord was not pleased. "The Lord came again unto the brother of Jared. . . . And for the space of three hours did the Lord talk with the brother of Jared, and *chastened him because he remembered not to call upon the name of the Lord.*"[9]

Mahonri immediately changed his ways. Because of an Atonement that stretches forward and backward to infinity, he was able to repent and turn his life around. Mahonri began to pray again. The Lord forgave him with a warning: "Thou shalt not sin any more, for ye shall remember that my Spirit will not always strive with man."[10]

How often have we made the same mistake? When our lives contain great challenges, we never miss a chance to pray, and we pray hard. After the Lord answers our prayers and leads us to a house on the spiritual beach, He somehow seems less important. We rely on the sun and the palm trees and the endless fish in the sea to sustain us. The wonderful things of the world slowly seduce us into trusting in them, and we pray less and less. Perhaps we subconsciously conclude that we won't bother the Lord because we don't really need Him that much anymore.

The warning of the Lord to Mahonri applies equally to us, "Wherefore, if ye will sin until ye are fully ripe ye shall be cut off

---

8   Ether 2:5.
9   Ether 2:14; emphasis added.
10   Ether 2:15.

from the presence of the Lord."[11] If we cut ourselves off from God by failing to pray to Him, at some point, He will cut us off from vital assistance we would otherwise receive. Whether this happens when we are toiling through the desert or relaxing on the beach, we are lost.

Mahonri never ceased to pray thereafter. He soon learned that it was time for the people of Jared to leave the beach. The Lord commanded them to build barges, and they obeyed.

As built, there were two problems with the barges—a lack of air and a lack of light. The brother of Jared prayed about both of these problems, and the Lord quickly gave him an answer to one, explaining how to modify the barges to provide air.

The Jaredites reworked the barges according to the Lord's instructions, and then the brother of Jared called on the Lord again. First, he reported that he had followed the Lord's directions, and then the brother of Jared prayed again about the absence of light inside the barges. The Lord answered this faith-filled prayer in a very interesting way: "What will ye that I should do that ye may have light in your vessels?"[12] The Lord then explained several possible solutions that would *not* work and asked, "Therefore what will ye that I should prepare for you that ye may have light when ye are swallowed up in the depths of the sea?"[13]

The Lord understood how the vessels could be lighted. He knew a thousand ways to light barges, but He withheld a solution. If He wanted the Jaredites to travel to the New World, why didn't the Lord just provide an immediate and understandable solution? The Lord was more interested in building Mahonri than He was in building barges.

How often in our lives does the Lord provide a similar response to our prayers so we can grow? If we erroneously believe that a "brother of Jared" answer to our prayers is no answer at all, we are making a mistake. The Lord *always* answers our prayers. Sometimes that answer will be much different from the one we expect, but if we begin with a firm faith that the Lord always answers our prayers, we will recognize many more divine responses, regardless of how surprising they may be to us.

---

11   Ether 2:15.

12   Ether 2:23.

13   Ether 2:25.

Although he didn't receive a solution when he prayed, Mahonri must have been nudged toward an answer by the Spirit. He climbed to a high mountain, obtained sixteen stones, and offered another powerful prayer for divine help of a very specific nature. "Therefore touch these stones, O Lord, with thy finger, and prepare them that they may shine forth in darkness; and they shall shine forth unto us in the vessels which we have prepared, that we may have light while we shall cross the sea."[14]

What happens next tells us something about why the Lord did not provide a simple answer to Mahonri's prior prayers and instead required that Mahonri increase his faith, "The Lord stretched forth his hand and touched the stones one by one with his finger. And the veil was taken from off the eyes of the brother of Jared, and he saw the finger of the Lord; and it was as the finger of a man, like unto flesh and blood."[15]

After Mahonri saw the finger of the Lord, "the Lord showed himself unto him, and said: Because thou knowest these things ye are redeemed from the fall; therefore ye are brought back into my presence; therefore I show myself unto you. . . . Behold, I am he who was prepared from the foundation of the world to redeem my people. Behold, I am Jesus Christ. I am the Father and the Son. In me shall all mankind have life, and that eternally."[16]

Mahonri prayed for the lighting of his ships and received the Light of the World. The Lord knew what He was doing when He responded to that heartfelt prayer in an unexpected way.

The Lord also gave a surprising answer to Oliver Cowdery's prayer that he be permitted to translate the gold plates.

Oliver was a mighty man, second only to Joseph Smith during the earliest days of the Restoration. Oliver received the Aaronic Priesthood under the hand of John the Baptist and was baptized by Joseph.[17] Joseph records, "No sooner had I baptized Oliver Cowdery, than the Holy Ghost fell upon him, and he stood up and prophesied

---

14   Ether 3:4.

15   Ether 3:6.

16   Ether 3:13–14.

17   Joseph Smith History (Salt Lake City, The Church of Jesus Christ of Latter-day Saints, 1989), 70–72.

many things which should shortly come to pass."[18] When the Church was organized, Oliver was called as "an apostle of Jesus Christ, to be the second elder of this church, and ordained under his hand."[19]

Two days after he met Joseph Smith, Oliver Cowdery began to assist Joseph in the translation of the Book of Mormon, transcribing as Joseph dictated. The translation proceeded faster than it ever had before. Oliver was a man selected by the Lord for a transcendent work, and he fulfilled his responsibilities well.

In April 1829, Oliver received marvelous promises in revelations recorded as Doctrine and Covenants 6 and 8. In Doctrine and Covenants 6, the Lord said, "Seek not for riches but for wisdom, and behold, the mysteries of God shall be unfolded unto you, and then shall you be made rich. Behold, he that hath eternal life is rich. Verily, verily, I say unto you, *even as you desire of me* so it shall be unto you; and *if you desire,* you shall be the means of doing much good in this generation."[20]

Oliver had prayed about translating the plates himself, doing the work Joseph was doing. In Doctrine and Covenants 6, the Lord responded. He first revealed that Oliver had the God-given capacity to translate and understand many great and marvelous spiritual truths, "Behold *thou hast a gift,* and blessed art thou because of thy gift. Remember it is sacred and cometh from above—And *if thou wilt inquire,* thou shalt know mysteries which are great and marvelous; therefore thou shalt exercise thy gift, that thou mayest find out mysteries."[21]

Then, the Lord answered Oliver's prayer by granting the gift of the power to translate the Book of Mormon active in Oliver's life, upon certain conditions, "And, behold, I grant unto you a gift, *if you desire of me,* to translate, even as my servant Joseph. Verily, verily, I say unto you, that there are records which contain much of my gospel, which have been kept back because of the wickedness of the people; And now I command you, *that if you have good desires—a desire to lay up treasures for yourself in heaven—*then shall you assist in bringing

---

18   Joseph Smith History, 73.

19   D&C 20:3.

20   D&C 6:7–8; emphasis added.

21   D&C 6:10–11; emphasis added.

to light, with your gift, those parts of my scriptures which have been hidden because of iniquity. And now, behold, I give unto you, and also unto my servant Joseph, the keys of this gift, which shall bring to light this ministry."[22]

In Doctrine and Covenants 8, Oliver received further promises and guidance regarding translation, "Oliver Cowdery, verily, verily, I say unto you, that assuredly as the Lord liveth, who is your God and your Redeemer, even so *surely shall you receive a knowledge of whatsoever things you shall ask in faith,* with an honest heart, believing that *you shall receive a knowledge concerning the engravings of old records,* which are ancient, which contain those parts of my scripture of which has been spoken by the manifestation of my Spirit. . . . Therefore *this is thy gift; apply unto it,* and blessed art thou. . . . Oh, *remember these words, and keep my commandments.* Remember, *this is your gift.*"[23]

The Lord then gives Oliver another great spiritual gift, the same gift that He gave Aaron, and then concludes the revelation by saying, "Remember that *without faith you can do nothing; therefore ask in faith. Trifle not with these things;* do not ask for that which you ought not. . . . And *according to your faith shall it be done unto you.*"[24]

Oliver was unable to translate and could not understand what was wrong. Joseph inquired of the Lord and received the revelation we know as Doctrine and Covenants 9 for Oliver, "Behold, I say unto you, my son, that . . . *you did not translate according to that which you desired of me.* . . . *Be patient,* my son, for *it is wisdom in me, and it is not expedient that you should translate at this present time.* Behold, the work which you are called to do is to write for my servant Joseph. And, behold, *it is because that you did not continue as you commenced,* when you began to translate, that I have taken away this privilege from you. Do not murmur, my son, for it is wisdom in me that I have dealt with you after this manner. Behold, *you have not understood; you have supposed that I would give it unto you, when you took no thought save it was to ask me.*"[25]

---

22 D&C 6:25–28; emphasis added.
23 D&C 8:1, 4–5; emphasis added.
24 D&C 8:10–11; emphasis added.
25 D&C 9:1, 3–7; emphasis added.

In contrast to the strenuous prayers and efforts of the brother of Jared, Oliver had not fulfilled the conditions the Lord set for exercising the gift of translation.

The Lord speaks to Oliver in a familiar, kind, and loving tone in Doctrine and Covenants sections 6 and 8. He knows of Oliver's many strengths and also of his weaknesses. The Lord gives Oliver careful instructions, instructions that acknowledge his strengths and provide direction on how to avoid his weak spiritual areas.

Just as you or I would be tempted to do, Oliver apparently treasured the wonderful gifts but paid less attention to the conditions under which those gifts could be exercised. We sense, when the Lord says, "Ye took no thought," that Oliver had become casual about his blessings. Perhaps he had "trifled" with those sacred opportunities. Perhaps Oliver had not "asked in faith" and had not "remembered the words" and conditions that the Lord had associated with Oliver's prior blessings.

We can learn by comparing the brother of Jared with Oliver. Each of these men was chosen of the Lord, greatly blessed and greatly loved. Each of these men had an important mission to perform in the Lord's kingdom. Each of these men prayed for something he desired very much.

But Mahonri did something different from what Oliver did. He did not take "no thought save it was to ask" the Lord. The brother of Jared worked to find a solution to his problem. The Lord had not provided an answer to his prayer by telling him what he should do, but He had provided valuable information about possible solutions that would not work. The brother of Jared understood that he needed to act before the Lord would provide further answers.

If we apply to the brother of Jared the standards the Lord set for Oliver Cowdery to use his gift to translate, we can understand something about the differing outcomes of the efforts of these two men to receive blessings:

- *If you have good desires—a desire to lay up treasures for yourself in heaven—*The brother of Jared desired to serve God and obey His commandments, and his actions demonstrated his desire. He began one prayer with the words, "O Lord, I have performed the work which thou hast commanded me."[26] His next prayer began with the words, "O Lord, behold I have done even as thou hast commanded me."[27]

- *Surely shall you receive a knowledge of whatsoever things you shall ask in faith*—When the brother of Jared approached the Lord to ask Him to touch the sixteen stones, he prayed intensely, "I know, O Lord, that thou hast all power, and can do whatsoever thou wilt for the benefit of man; therefore touch these stones, O Lord, with thy finger, and prepare them that they may shine forth in darkness. . . . Behold, O Lord, thou canst do this. We know that thou art able to show forth great power."[28] Mahonri had no doubt that the Lord had the power to perform a much-needed miracle, and his great faith in that power is evident.

- *Remember these words, and keep my commandments*—After the brother of Jared received the word of the Lord on how to modify the vessels to provide air, Moroni records simply, "And it came to pass that the brother of Jared did so, according as the Lord had commanded."[29] As he offers the prayer that will lead him to see the finger of the Lord, Mahonri says, "O Lord, thou hast given us a commandment that we must call upon thee, that from thee we may receive according to our desires."[30]

Second Nephi 25:23 reads, "We know that it is by grace that we are saved, after all we can do." When you consider the "all we can do" requirement of salvation, think of the keys the Lord gave to Oliver and how your prayers and your works combine to access the promises these keys can unlock: "If you have good desires—a desire to lay up treasures for yourself in heaven,"[31] "surely shall you receive a

---

26   Ether 2:18.
27   Ether 2:22.
28   Ether 3:4–5.
29   Ether 2:21.
30   Ether 3:2.
31   D&C 6:27.

knowledge of whatsoever things you shall ask in faith."[32] "Remember these words, and keep my commandments."[33]

The "all that we can do" portion of this divine equation requires regular heartfelt prayers. A prayer that includes a spoken or unspoken reservation will not work. We cannot say to ourselves, "I'll see what Heavenly Father says and then decide what I will do." "All we can do" requires a willingness to act upon any answer the Lord gives us, to wait patiently for an answer or sometimes to act upon our existing knowledge when the Lord indicates no preference about a particular decision. "All we can do" requires significant study and thought concerning *what* we should do and *how* we should proceed along whatever path God desires us to follow. Sometimes it requires the prayerful intensity exemplified by the brother of Jared.

We pray with power when we make all the necessary effort to do our part. Once we do that, the Lord will take us the rest of the way along our individual path to exaltation. The celestial kingdom is not for wimps. The effect of our every interaction with the Atonement should be that we are stronger afterward than we were before. We pray with the understanding that the Lord's kind and wise answers will include our stretching farther than we thought we could stretch, bearing more than we thought we could bear, changing more than we thought we could change, loving more than we thought we could love.

As we pray and as we obey, we can rely upon our Heavenly Father and our Savior to do Their work with us and to bring to pass our eternal life. But a casual or trifling attitude is not what They seek from us. We must commit all that we are. When we receive an answer to our prayers, we can know that this answer will in some way lead us closer to eternal life even if the answer is unexpected. When we pray and do not seem to receive an answer, we can know that this experience will lead us closer to eternal life if we will permit it to do so. Our Father and our Savior will save us if we allow Them to do so. They are always focused on our salvation.

Our journey toward eternal life, the sanctification that is the greatest gift of the Atonement, isn't accomplished with one prayer or two. For most of us, humble, faith-filled prayers must be innumerable.

---

32   D&C 8:1.

33   D&C 8:5.

We have so far to travel, and we must be changed so much by our Savior's love that it is not surprising that receiving this unimaginable blessing will take time and require all of our heart.

Because of the Atonement, however, we can pray along with the brother of Jared, "Behold, O Lord, thou canst do this. We know that thou art able to show forth great power."[34]

Abide with me! fast falls the eventide;
The darkness deepens. Lord, with me abide!
When other helpers fail and comforts flee,
Help of the helpless, oh, abide with me!

I need thy presence ev'ry passing hour.
What but thy grace can foil the tempter's pow'r?
Who, like thyself, my guide and stay can be?
Thru cloud and sunshine, Lord, abide with me!

—"Abide with Me!" *Hymns,* no. 166

---

34 Ether 3:5.

HAYSTACKS AND CARDBOARD WINGS—THE FALL AND THE ATONEMENT

I don't care what they say with
their mouths—everybody knows that
something *is eternal. And it ain't houses and it ain't*
names, and it ain't earth, and it ain't even the stars. . . .
Everybody knows in their bones that something *is eternal, and*
that something has to do with human beings. All the greatest
people ever lived have been telling us that for five thousand
years and yet you'd be surprised how people are always
losing hold of it. There's something way down deep
that's eternal about every human being.

—Stage Manager, in Thornton Wilder, *Our Town* (New York: HarperCollins, 2003)

Why include the Fall in a book about applying the Atonement in our daily lives? The Fall is central to our daily challenges and the daily uses that we make of the Atonement. Without the Fall, I don't know that we would have needed the Atonement, at least not as desperately. When Adam and Eve fell, the whole world and everything in it fell. All day, every day, we deal with the consequences of living as fallen beings in a fallen world. These consequences are the source of many of the frustrations we feel in this life.

We were obedient in the preexistence, but now we find it more difficult to consistently obey Heavenly Father's commandments. All around us we see a mortal world in which good doesn't appear to be rewarded and evil seems to triumph, a situation we can't imagine occurring in the immediate presence of God. The Fall often makes us feel weaker than the challenges that face us.

Many, if not most, of the tests of this life have their origin in consequence of the Fall. By virtue of the Fall, we experience an impairment of the abilities and knowledge that were formerly ours. We are separated from the immediate presence of Heavenly Father and Jesus Christ, who are the source of our strength, happiness, and hope. Our conscious memories of premortal life and all we learned there are hidden behind a veil. We don't even remember choosing to come to earth. Our physical senses testify that mortal birth is the beginning and mortal death is the end of our lives. We can only read about immortality and eternal life without being able to observe it.

The Fall has left us with only a subset of the abilities we formerly possessed and will enjoy in the future. For example, we retain the ability to develop and exercise our faith. This attribute was less important to us when we could see and hear our Heavenly Father and Jesus but now is central to our relationship with Them. I do not know what characterized our association with the Holy Ghost in the preexistence, but today we must vigilantly listen for His still, small voice to hear what God and Christ would have us do.

The full development of the spiritual abilities we retain in mortality and the use we make of them is essential to our growth into the next stage of our lives. The most important of all of our earth-life capabilities is our freedom to draw upon the power of the Atonement of Jesus Christ.

Elder Bruce R. McConkie said, "The three pillars of eternity, the three events, preeminent and transcendent above all others, are the creation, the fall, and the atonement. These three are the foundations upon which all things rest. Without any one of them, all things would lose their purpose and meaning, and the plans and designs of Deity would come to naught."[1]

We need the Fall and all the constraints and trials it brings to us. This mortal earth is not our permanent home, but it is an essential stop on the path that will lead us there. There are tests we must face in this

---

1　"The Three Pillars of Eternity," devotional address given at Brigham Young University on 17 Feb. 1981.

place, tests that require a fallen body, tests that require separation from the physical presence of our Heavenly Father, tests that require a Savior.

FLYING

When I was six years old, I believed I could fly.

I had a series of vivid dreams in which I was flying. It was wonderful. I still remember with pleasure my dream experience when I simply lifted off the ground into effortless and graceful flight. I flew to my school. I took my friends flying, and it was wonderful to be up in the sky in the sunshine looking down at the beautiful earth.

After those dreams, I wanted to fly. Lifting off the ground appeared to be my biggest challenge, so I needed to be up in the air to get a good start; then the rest of flying would come naturally.

Like most ranches, ours had rectangular hay bales piled into a haystack. This was the perfect place to conduct my flight training. I climbed to the top of the haystack and focused my six-year-old mind on the process of flying—how to jump into the air and then move upward. Resolutely concentrating my thoughts on this task would be the key to my success. The power to fly was somewhere inside me. I just had to perfect it.

I walked over to the edge of the haystack and looked down. Holding my thoughts of flight firmly in my mind, I backed up a few steps and ran as fast as I could toward the edge of the haystack. I planted my foot, looked up toward the sky, and made a mighty leap into the air.

I flew. Or it seemed to me that I flew. I thought I could feel myself moving up a little, becoming weightless like I would be in flight. Then I fell to the ground. Fortunately, some loose hay lay at the base of the haystack.

Now I understood flying even better. The art of flying as I could in my dreams meant grabbing hold of that instant when I felt myself going up and not letting go. I climbed back to the top of the haystack and put myself into a flying state of mind, focusing hard on extending my brief period of flight. I ran to the edge of the haystack. Once again, I felt the beginnings of flight. However, I was unable to extend those beginnings and fell once again.

I enhanced my flying concentration by reciting the words from the television show *Superman*. Superman was very accomplished at flying. As I ran toward the edge of the haystack, I said, "It's a bird, it's a plane, it's Superman!" I jumped just as I said, "It's Superman!"

That didn't work, either. I needed to think more about my takeoff, and my feet were a little sore, so I stopped.

The next day, I marched to the haystack with a blanket. I had seen paratroopers in movies with their parachutes. My blanket parachute would be like training wheels, steadying me until I became really good at flying.

Arranging my blanket like a parachute, I focused my thoughts, repeated my Superman mantra, and jumped into the air. I seemed to stay up just a little longer, but my blanket didn't work. I climbed the haystack again, vowing to hold my blanket properly this time so I could stay up in the air. After a few more tries, I concluded that a blanket wasn't the answer. Then I made an important discovery—wings.

The next day I went to the haystack with wings I had carefully cut from a cardboard box. I had one cardboard wing under each arm, attached with string. My invention would allow me to either fly with fixed wings, like an airplane, or flap my wings like a bird. It was an ideal arrangement.

Holding my cardboard wings so they would catch the air, I carefully visualized Superman, ran to the edge of the haystack, and once again cherished that first moment of flight. Then the wings made my arms go straight up, smacking both sides of my head as I fell. When I landed, one knee bumped me hard on the chin. I could taste a little blood in my mouth, and my feet were sore again, so I stopped.

For several days thereafter, I held on to my hopes for flight, but no more flying dreams came in the night, and my cardboard wings gathered dust in our garage.

THE UPWARD PULL

President David O. McKay once said, "Man is a spiritual being, a soul, and at some period of his life everyone is possessed with an irresistible desire to know his relationship to the Infinite. . . . There is something within him which urges him to rise above himself, to control his environment, to master the body and all things physical and live in a higher and more beautiful world."[2]

Although we have a veil drawn across our understanding of the premortal life with our Heavenly Father, the spirit that inhabits our mortal body is the same spirit that walked in the gardens and palaces of the God of the universe. That association changed our spirit permanently. We may smother and enfeeble that spirit with sin, but we cannot remove those experiences. Who we are now, who we really are in our best moments, is a direct extension of who we were when we shouted for joy when our brother Jesus agreed to be our Savior.

The veil is firmly in place, but like the compass needle that trembles back and forth before pointing unerringly at an unseen North Pole thousands of miles away, our spirits are drawn to our heavenly home where we once dwelled and to our Heavenly Father whose love is a beacon stretching across an unimaginable distance to turn our hearts toward Him. Just as tiny salmon hatchlings are swept downstream and into a immense ocean only to fight past incredible obstacles, always moving upward, ever swimming against the current, to unerringly return to the place where they were born, we know this earth is not our real home. We know the pathway back is a spiritual path, and to walk upon it, we need to move upstream. We want to return to that higher and more beautiful world that we cannot see because its absence we sometimes feel intensely.

We sense the direction of our real home, but where is the road that will lead us there? When we sometimes struggle to survive a single hour or day, how will we find the strength for such an impossible journey? How can we possibly rise so far?

> Yea, come unto Christ, and *be perfected in him,* and deny yourselves of all ungodliness; and if ye shall deny yourselves of all ungodliness, and love God with all your might, mind and strength, *then is his grace sufficient for you,* that by his grace ye may be perfect

---

2   *True to the Faith: From the Sermons and Discourses of David O. McKay,* comp. Llewelyn R. McKay [1966], 244.

in Christ; and if by the grace of God ye are perfect in Christ, ye can in nowise deny the power of God.

And again, *if ye by the grace of God are perfect in Christ, and deny not his power, then are ye sanctified in Christ by the grace of God,* through the shedding of the blood of Christ, which is in the covenant of the Father unto the remission of your sins, *that ye become holy, without spot.*[3]

Even though we are mortal, we all want to fly, to overcome the limitations of our mortal selves, to rise up and view broader, more beautiful vistas that we sense are somewhere above us, somewhere we used to live. Buried deep beneath our memories is a feeling that we are capable of so much more than we can accomplish on this earth. When we are paying attention, we feel that upward pull to be a better person in a better place. This better person seems more like our genuine self than the person we are now does. We want to become that better person, and we want to be in that better place, but we cannot do it by ourselves.

Mortal life paints a heavy disguise over our true beings. We want to move upward, but we keep falling. Only through the grace of our Savior can we discover what lies beneath that disguise.

We can't understand the necessity of the Atonement unless we understand the Fall. We can't understand our mortal lives and all that happens to us here unless we understand the Fall.

As Thou Hast Fallen Thou Mayest Be Redeemed

When Adam and Eve were first in the Garden of Eden, they enjoyed the presence of Heavenly Father and Jesus. Adam and Eve could see and hear Them with their physical eyes and ears. They basked in the wonderful influence of being physically near these Heavenly Beings. That physical association made a strong spiritual connection easy and natural.

---

3   Moroni 10:32–33; emphasis added.

When Adam and Eve transgressed, they were cast out of their idyllic garden home. More significantly, they were physically separated from their Father and their Elder Brother.

By the Fall, Adam and Eve and the whole earth became mortal. By obtaining knowledge of good and evil, Adam and Eve could knowingly choose either good or evil with their physical bodies. Mortal bodies died. Mortal beings could commit sin, and all but our Savior did. Since no unclean thing could be in the presence of God, Adam, Eve, and all of their children could no longer enjoy that physical closeness with Him.

The Fall brought a separation from God, a spiritual death. This separation was part of the greatest test. Would Adam and Eve choose good over evil when they were no longer in the physical presence of God, when they were living in mortal bodies and were required to constrain their carnal desires, appetites, and passions?

I have not found anything in the scriptures that indicates Adam and Eve had the same veil of forgetfulness drawn across their memories when they were cast out of the Garden of Eden as is drawn across ours when we are born. What agony Adam and Eve must have felt at their separation from their Heavenly Father and their Savior. What an immense emptiness they must have felt remembering their divine associations and blessings but now being deprived of those associations.

For a time, at least, they were able to hear the Lord's voice, but they could not see Him. "Adam and Eve, his wife, called upon the name of the Lord, and they heard the voice of the Lord from the way toward the Garden of Eden, speaking unto them, and they saw him not; for they were shut out from his presence."[4] That is the last record that indicates Adam and Eve heard the voice of the Lord coming from a specific earthly place. Shortly thereafter, an angel appeared to Adam as he was offering sacrifices as the Lord had commanded.[5] At this time, Adam and Eve received the Holy Ghost and an important message.

> And in that day the Holy Ghost fell upon Adam,
> which beareth record of the Father and the Son,

---

4   Moses 5:4.

5   See Moses 5:6.

saying: I am the Only Begotten of the Father from the beginning, henceforth and forever, that *as thou hast fallen thou mayest be redeemed*, and all mankind, even as many as will. And in that day Adam blessed God and was filled, and began to prophesy concerning all the families of the earth, saying: Blessed be the name of God, for because of my transgression my eyes are opened, and *in this life I shall have joy, and again in the flesh I shall see God.* And Eve, his wife, heard all these things and was glad, saying: Were it not for our transgression we never should have had seed, and never should have known good and evil, and the joy of our redemption, and *the eternal life which God giveth unto all the obedient.*[6]

The Holy Ghost was sent to minister to Adam and Eve's spirits, now captive for a season inside mortal bodies. The Holy Ghost could speak spirit to spirit. The Holy Ghost could change mortal souls, he could sanctify them, transform them into more Christlike beings. He brought the possibility of redemption through the Atonement of Christ.

Just as Adam and Eve made a choice that led to their mortality, each of us made that same choice when we agreed to leave our premortal home and come to earth in a mortal body. That choice meant that we too suffered a spiritual death, separated from the physical presence of God.

Although the veil over our memories may have blunted the agony of separation Adam and Eve may have experienced, the upward pull that we feel is the same pull that Adam and Eve felt to return to the presence of their Heavenly Father. At times, we also feel an empty place in our hearts that was formerly filled by our wonderful and intimate association with our Father and our Savior.

We also received the Holy Ghost as a counselor and guide to our spirits. Mortality would be a test of whether we would listen to that still, small voice and obey God's commandments when we could not see Him and hear His voice directly.

---

6   Moses 5:9–11; emphasis added.

The Fall and its hardships are essential to God's plan and our possibilities. We had reached the end of our potential for growth and development living in our heavenly home. We only had spirit bodies there. We needed to learn how to live in and control a physical body.

The Great Test

Just like my flying experiments, controlling a physical body is easier in theory than in practice. How often we all relearn the truth that "the spirit indeed is willing, but the flesh is weak."[7]

Our mortal bodies are very demanding. Even though they are destined to die, our bodies require air, water, food, and protection from extreme weather so they can continue to live. When any of these necessities is lacking, it is difficult for us to think of anything except satisfying the immediate demands of our body. For example, if we stay under water for a period of time, all our thoughts are directed toward our next breath of air and preserving our physical life. This demanding nature can make a mortal body today seem far more important than an eternal body tomorrow.

Our bodies make other demands, demands not necessary to continue mortal life. These demands are temptations to do evil. From pride to envy to lasciviousness and a thousand other things, such temptations are regularly present, at least to some degree. Satan tries to convince us that he offers shortcuts to the happiness and fulfillment our spirits desire. He slyly suggests that the spiritual emptiness and longing we sometimes feel can be filled with physical experiences. Thus our bodies may seem to demand sinful thoughts and behavior as urgently as they press us for air or water.

What strange creatures we are, a sometimes uncomfortable combination of the physical and the spiritual. Our physical bodies don't always fit our spirits very well. Our spirits are pure because they have heavenly parents. But our spirits are tied to mortal bodies assembled from the components of a fallen earth. Our spirits want to fly, and our bodies want to fall.

This condition sets up the great test. Which will be in control, our spirit or our body? Either is capable of dominating the other. We experience a constant tension, a ceaseless contest.

---

7   Matt. 26:41.

Our physical bodies sometimes win. We are unkind or envious. We steal a glance at something we know we should not look at. There are a thousand ways, little and large, for our mortal half to draw us away from heaven. When our physical selves control our behavior, we are natural men and women, a condition that places us in opposition to God and His hopes for us, "For the natural man is an enemy to God, and has been from the fall of Adam, and will be, forever and ever, unless he yields to the enticings of the Holy Spirit, and putteth off the natural man."[8] We don't really want to be enemies of God, but without direction from our spirit, our mortal body keeps putting us on the wrong side of His commandments.

When we yield to temptations to do evil, we place ourselves under the increasing influence of that being who is the source of all such temptations. Satan rebelled against God long ago and has battled with Him ever since. That battle takes on many forms, but it is always for the same stakes—the souls of men and women. If Satan can direct a physical body, he can enslave the spirit within.

C. S. Lewis captured the nature of our mortal tendency to oppose God when he wrote, "Fallen man is not simply an imperfect creature who needs improvement; he is a rebel who must lay down his arms."[9]

Just as the Fall separates man from God, it also separates man from man. In the presence of a common spiritual Father, it is easy for us to recognize that we are all brothers and sisters. In mortality, natural men and women are tempted to look upon the bodies of some of their brothers and sisters with disdain, dislike, or even hatred. Satan seizes on meaningless differences to set men against one another. We can and do harm one another both physically and spiritually.

The spiritual harm comes because our spirits cannot be separated from our bodies so long as we live. As our physical bodies commit sins, our pure spirits are battered and abused. Just as our physical bodies will weaken if not properly cared for and nourished, our spirits decline in strength when they do not receive proper spiritual sustenance. Our spirits suffer acute, sometimes debilitating injuries when they are exposed to the excruciating injury of serious sin.

---

8   Mosiah 3:19.

9   C. S. Lewis, *Mere Christianity* (New York: Harper One, 2001), 59.

The Need for the Atonement

In contrast to all the separation inherent in the Fall, the Atonement joins us again. The Atonement brings man back together with God. The Atonement transforms the relationship of man to man from one characterized by pride, envy, and exploitation by drawing us upward toward our Savior and, in the process, bringing us closer to one another and showing us our brotherhood. We cannot truly love our Lord and hate our brother.

Because we have a loving Heavenly Father, His plan includes a means of overcoming the Fall, including salvation from physical death and salvation from spiritual death—a way to return to Him. This plan required a Savior, Jesus Christ.

Paul writes, "For as in Adam all die, even so in Christ shall all be made alive."[10]

The Atonement of Christ brings about the resurrection of all men and women, transforming their dead mortal bodies into physical bodies that will not die and joining those bodies to their immortal spirits to live forever. One of the results of our mortal test is that *the immortal physical bodies we receive will match the spirits we have developed during mortality.* Unlike our mortal experience when the body and spirit sometimes pull in opposite directions, our resurrected bodies will fit perfectly with our spirits. Thus, Christ overcomes the physical death that came with the Fall.

Amulek testifies, "The spirit and the body shall be reunited again in its perfect form; both limb and joint shall be restored to its proper frame, even as we now are at this time."[11] "Perfect form," or "proper frame," to me, describes a condition in which our outside matches our inside. Each of us knows men and women who have built a wonderful spirit within what many would call an impaired body. In a celestial sense, each of us has an impaired body while living in mortality, a body that will die and require resurrection. Our spirit is already immortal. It does not require a resurrection. Because "the Lord looketh on the heart,"[12] He will make certain that our resurrected body perfectly conforms to our spirit.

10   1 Cor. 15:22.
11   Alma 11:43.
12   1 Sam. 16:7.

Alma taught his son Corianton a vivid lesson about the reunion of an immortal physical body and an immortal spirit body upon resurrection:

> And it is requisite with the justice of God that men should be judged according to their works; and if their works were good in this life, and the desires of their hearts were good, that they should also, at the last day, be restored unto that which is good.
>
> And if their works are evil they shall be restored unto them for evil. Therefore, all things shall be restored to their proper order, every thing to its natural frame—mortality raised to immortality, corruption to incorruption—raised to endless happiness to inherit the kingdom of God, or to endless misery to inherit the kingdom of the devil, the one on one hand, the other on the other—
>
> The one raised to happiness according to his desires of happiness, or good according to his desires of good; and the other to evil according to his desires of evil; for as he has desired to do evil all the day long even so shall he have his reward of evil when the night cometh. . . .
>
> And now behold, is the meaning of the word restoration to take a thing of a natural state and place it in an unnatural state, or to place it in a state opposite to its nature?
>
> O, my son, this is not the case; but the meaning of the word restoration is to bring back again evil for evil, or carnal for carnal, or devilish for devilish— good for that which is good; righteous for that which is righteous; just for that which is just; merciful for that which is merciful.[13]

I once heard a man speak about glimpsing a resurrected celestial body. When some men reach middle age, they become stupid. This

---

13   Alma 41:3–5, 12–13.

man had become dissatisfied with many aspects of his life and focused his dissatisfaction on his wife. He felt that she was not as physically attractive as she had been when they married. He unwisely shared these feelings with his wife and hurt her deeply. Understandably, she withdrew from him.

The man's thoughts began to wander dangerously, as did his eyes. As he moved closer and closer to a terrible mistake, a merciful Lord intervened.

One night, as the man was sleeping, he began to dream of a wonderful place. This place was full of light, and the man observed beautiful palaces and stunning gardens. As the man tried to comprehend the incredible splendor he was viewing, he saw a bright figure walking toward him. The figure was wearing a long flowing white robe and was surrounded by a brilliant light. As the figure drew closer, the man was astounded at its perfection and beauty.

Soon, the person drew close enough for the man to discern that the figure was a woman. At first, the light from her face made it difficult to recognize her features. But when the woman stopped and greeted him, the man instantly recognized his wife. Then the dream faded.

In the morning, the man humbly went to his wife. A sincere apology was offered and accepted. As the man spoke of his experience, he said he had not previously understood who his wife really was. Thereafter, he never looked at her without remembering how she appeared in her celestial glory, with a body that perfectly matched her spirit. He could not bear the thought that he might be separated from her.

Overcoming Spiritual Death

Perhaps the single most important point to understand about the Fall and our need for the Atonement is that it is impossible for us to save ourselves. We cannot cleanse ourselves from our own sins, and we cannot return to our Heavenly Father without a Savior and Guide. We cannot establish our own righteousness any more than we can flap cardboard wings and fly.

Paul writes, "Brethren, my heart's desire and prayer to God for Israel is, that they might be saved. . . . For they being ignorant of God's righteousness, and *going about to establish their own righteousness, have not submitted themselves unto the righteousness of God.* For Christ is the end of the law for righteousness to every one that believeth.[14] Samuel the Lamanite preaches the same great truth from the walls of Zarahemla, "And if ye believe on his [Christ's] name ye will repent of all your sins, that thereby ye may have a remission of them *through his merits.*"[15] Lehi said with perfect clarity, "All mankind were in a lost and in a fallen state, *and ever would be save they should rely on this Redeemer.*"[16]

There are many members of the Church who work hard to be righteous. If we were to rank all of mankind, from the least to the most obedient, faithful, and righteous, surely many Latter-day Saints would be arrayed among the ranks of the most righteous.

But it is not enough. Even the second most righteous person ever to walk this earth in mortality cannot save himself or herself. We cannot atone for even one of our sins in such a way as to remove its permanent effects on us.

When I was six years old, I am certain that I was among the most expert and skilled boys in the world at unaided human flight. My mind was purely and completely focused on flight. There were few that were better than I was at flying.

But however great my skills, however clear my vision, however meticulous my preparation, nothing I could do was sufficient to allow me to fly. No matter how hard I tried, I was earthbound. I could look up to the sky and envision myself there, but, worlds without end, I could not go there by myself.

We need a Savior to return to our Heavenly Father. We can't even come close without Jesus Christ. Sheri Dew wrote, "The Savior isn't our last chance; He is our only chance. Our only chance to overcome self-doubt and catch a vision of who we may become. Our only chance to repent and have our sins washed clean. Our only chance to purify our hearts, subdue our weaknesses, and avoid the adversary. Our only chance to obtain redemption and exaltation. Our only chance to find peace and happiness in this life and eternal life in the world to come."[17]

---

14   Rom. 10:1, 3–4; emphasis added.

15   Hel. 14:13; emphasis added.

16   1 Ne. 10:6; emphasis added.

17   "Our Only Chance," *Ensign,* May 1999, 66–67; emphasis in original.

A Broken Heart and a Contrite Spirit

Does this mean that we can't do anything about our sins and shortcomings? No, it does not. *Without Jesus Christ,* we can't do anything about our sins and shortcomings. *With Jesus Christ,* the story is wonderfully different. Because we have a Savior, through His Atonement, our sins can be removed. And we don't have to wait until we die for this miracle to occur. We can be clean and pure before our Heavenly Father both on this day and on Judgment Day.

Even though our Savior is the key to our salvation, He asks us to obey His commandments. Even when our own effort isn't even close to being enough, we are required to do all that we can to be righteous. We must stretch just as high as our puny mortal selves can stretch. We have to give our all even as the Savior has given His all.

Robert Millet has written, "The gospel is in fact a covenant—a two-way promise. The Lord agrees to do for us what we could never do for ourselves—forgive our sins, lift our burdens, renew our souls and re-create our nature, raise us from the dead, and qualify us for glory hereafter. At the same time, we promise to do what we *can* do: receive the ordinances of salvation, love and serve one another, and do all in our power to put off the natural man and deny ourselves of ungodliness."[18]

Where do we find this covenant, this "two-way promise," that governs the application of the Atonement in our lives? The promise flows throughout the scriptures and has repeatedly been taught by prophets and apostles. One of my favorite expressions of the covenant is in Mosiah 18:8–10:

> And it came to pass that he said unto them: Behold, here are the waters of Mormon (for thus were they called) and now, as *ye are desirous to come into the fold of God,* and to be called his people, and are *willing to bear one another's burdens,* that they may be light;
>
> Yea, and are willing to *mourn with those that mourn;* yea, and *comfort those that stand in need of comfort,* and to *stand as witnesses* of God at all times

---

18   *Grace Works* (Salt Lake City: Deseret Book, 2007), 116; emphasis in original.

and in all things, and in all places that ye may be in, even until death, *that ye may be redeemed of God,* and be numbered with those of the first resurrection, *that ye may have eternal life—*

Now I say unto you, if this be the desire of your hearts, what have you against being baptized in the name of the Lord, as a witness before him that *ye have entered into a covenant with him,* that *ye will serve him* and *keep his commandments,* that he may pour out his Spirit more abundantly upon you?

To be clear, good works evidence our faith, our desire to remain in covenant with Christ. But these good works, though *necessary* for our salvation, *are not sufficient to save us.*

Only the great gift of Christ's Atonement is sufficient to save us. *He never owes us this gift. We have never earned this gift.* Worlds without end, we cannot do enough to earn this gift because the gift is too great, impossibly out of proportion to our ability to pay for it. We receive this gift *only* because of His great love and mercy toward us.

The tiny thing that Christ asks of us in return for His gift is that we obey His commandments. It is not tiny to us, but it is tiny in comparison to what we receive in return. The beginning of obedience almost always involves a broken heart and a contrite spirit, "Thou shalt offer a sacrifice unto the Lord thy God in righteousness, even that of a broken heart and a contrite spirit."[19]

How often do we make this sacrifice? Every day. When we do so, a deep humility settles upon us. Pride recedes before a broken heart and contrite spirit. Pride can be difficult to eradicate, but it withers in such a spiritual environment. With humility comes wanting only what the Lord wants. How could anything be better than what the Lord wants?

If what we want is different from what the Lord wants, we must be wrong. This error calls for repentance and a realignment of the desires of our hearts with what the Lord desires. That realignment will always bring us peace, a quiet confidence that, although we may feel unequal

---

19   D&C 59:8.

to the challenges of our world, the Lord can overcome any challenges. When our path is His path, we can meekly travel in His wake.

President Joseph Fielding Smith has summarized the relationship between God's grace and our works by discussing the teachings of Paul and of James:

> So Paul taught these people—*who thought that they could be saved by some power that was within them,* or by observing the law of Moses—he pointed out to them the fact that if it were not for the mission of Jesus Christ, if it were not for this great atoning sacrifice, they could not be redeemed. And therefore it was by *the grace of God* that they are saved, *not by any work on their part,* for they were absolutely helpless. Paul was absolutely right.
>
> And on the other hand, James taught just as the Lord taught, just as Paul had taught in other scripture, that *it is our duty, of necessity, to labor, to strive in diligence, and faith, keeping the commandments of the Lord,* if we would obtain that inheritance which is promised to the faithful. . . .
>
> So it is easy to understand that we must accept the mission of Jesus Christ. We must believe that *it is through his grace that we are saved, that he performed for us that labor which we were unable to perform for ourselves, and did for us those things which were essential to our salvation, which were beyond our power; and also that we are under the commandment and the necessity of performing the labors that are required of us* as set forth in the commandments known as the gospel of Jesus Christ.[20]

So we live here in mortality striving to maintain this strange balance. We must obey and work as hard as we can if we are to be saved, knowing while we do so that our own efforts fall pitifully short of what is necessary. As we come to know our Heavenly Father and

---

20 *Doctrines of Salvation: Sermons and Writings of Joseph Fielding Smith,* comp Bruce R. McConkie (Salt Lake City: Bookcraft, 1954), 2:310–11; emphasis added.

our Savior better through our obedience to their commandments, it becomes clearer and clearer to us that we are millions and millions and millions of miles below them in virtue and capability.

C. S. Lewis wrote, "In one sense the road back to God is a road of moral effort, of trying harder and harder. But in another sense it is not trying that is ever going to bring us home. All this trying leads up to the vital moment at which you turn to God and say, 'You must do this. I can't.'"[21]

Moving Away and Turning Back

One of the overriding characteristics of man living in a fallen world separated from God is that we commit sins over and over. If we are diligently striving to live righteously, even though our sins may be small, they are all the more frustrating because we understand something about how high God's standards are.

At times we feel like we are finally moving to a permanent, higher plateau in our personal behavior and obedience, and then we do something stupid. A critical thought enters our mind, and the thoughtless word slips from our tongue so quickly and so easily that we despair that we can ever become better.

The Latin root word for *transgress* means "to cross over" or "to move away." There is more than one Hebrew word used to describe the concept of repentance. Sometimes the word *nacham* is used. This means "to sigh heavily" or "to be sorry." Another Hebrew term often used in the Old Testament is the word *shuv* or *shub*. This word means "to turn," "to return," or "to turn back."

When I was first learning how to drive, it seemed to me that when I was on a straight road, I should be able to get the car moving in a straight line and then just hold the steering wheel still and travel to my destination. I soon learned that no matter how accurately I aligned the car with the highway and how carefully I held the steering wheel, driving down a straight road involved making constant small corrections with the steering wheel as the car began to drift in one direction or the other, slightly off my centered course.

---

21   *Mere Christianity*, 146.

Only small corrections were necessary when I was on the right road and going in the right direction. If I made a significant error, it was sometimes necessary to turn the wheel sharply to avoid driving off the road and into a ditch. If I was on the wrong road, much larger corrections were necessary. Sometimes a ninety-degree turn was required, and at other times, I needed to make a U-turn and travel in exactly the opposite direction.

Many airplanes have an autopilot system. Once the autopilot is set with a course and altitude, it will adjust the aircraft's controls to hold the plane on that course and altitude until the autopilot is disengaged or the plane runs out of fuel. Sophisticated autopilot systems can be programmed to fly to a specific airport. These systems adjust the aircraft's controls to account for the wind's effect and some can even reduce altitude at the proper time to prepare the plane for landing at its destination.

Wouldn't an autopilot be wonderful for our lives? With such a system, we could designate our destination, the celestial kingdom, and then sit back while the autopilot automatically steered us to that destination. If the winds of adversity blew, our autopilot would automatically adjust our course so we would arrive at the right place. Unfortunately, our lives are more like driving an automobile.

As we move down life's road, even if we're on a straight and narrow path, we drift a little. We commit small transgressions that move us away from God. If we're good spiritual drivers, we quickly acknowledge the problem and repent, turning back to our Heavenly Father, bringing ourselves back on His highway to heaven. Just as with an automobile, it's much easier to make frequent small adjustments than it is to jerk the steering wheel just before we go into a ditch.

Even when we are living righteously, a fallen world is ceaselessly eroding our faith and testimony. When we allow good things to slide out of our lives, evil things will inevitably slide in to replace them. Would that it were evil being constantly undermined instead of good, but then the test would be too easy.

This frequent adjusting, this repenting of our sins to constantly realign ourselves with our Savior, is central to our mortal lives, something so important to our spiritual development that we are never free from doing it. If we believe that many years of repenting ought to earn us a vacation from continuing to do so, we've misunderstood how vital every mile of our journey is to the destination we must reach. If we look at someone else and think that he or she seems to have an easier journey than we do and that somehow we're entitled to some compensation for our different, harder road, we're missing the point of what we're here to do and to become.

We cannot arrive at our desired destination on our own, no matter how carefully we drive. It is too far, and we could never understand, let alone follow, the directions necessary to get there. Our daily drive is a demonstration to our Savior that we are willing to keep His commandments and remember Him and take His name upon us. He has asked us to drive and adjust our course, not so we can arrive at the end of our journey through our own means of transportation but so that we can qualify for Him to take us there.

Elaine Shaw Sorensen has written about the nature of our journey and its relationship to a future eternal life:

> Grace transcends mortal rules of justice. Life is not a mechanical scale of effort or suffering on one side balanced by the appropriate reward on the other. *Life is a process of growth, where growth itself becomes the reward.* I tired long ago of hearing promises of some future mortal reward equal to my suffering, as when well-meaning friends foresee financial security or loving companionship in a future whose happiness will outweigh the sadness of my past. The deceiving logic of such an idea implies that when life goes on, droning with problems, with no glory in sight, I am not yet worthy or perhaps have not yet suffered enough. That is unsettling, when all around, those apparently less righteous or less tried seem to be reaping the glorious gifts of this earth.
>
> The fact is that trials are neither distributed equally nor sorted according to a subsequent and matching earthly or heavenly treasure. Problems are neither price nor penance for credit toward some misconceived idea of payment. *Instead, life itself, even eternal life, with growth, hope, and peace promised by the Savior's atonement,*

becomes its own reward, offering divine gifts of the Spirit. The proving question is not What will I gain or achieve? but Who will I become?[22]

Bringing the Atonement's blessings and power into our lives every day includes constantly noticing and repenting of small sins. In a world that teaches tolerance of the ugliest practices, it can be difficult to acknowledge the small sins. If we are looking to the fallen world to identify such sins, they won't be acknowledged. If we are daily drawing close to our Heavenly Father and seeking for the Spirit's guidance and companionship in our common hours, we will be prompted to change, prompted to repent, prompted to grow, and we will receive the strength to do these things.

Robert Millet wrote,

> Life is repentance . . . progression and improvement and growth and maturity and refinement are all forms of repentance . . . the God-fearing live in a constant state of repentance. It is not intended that we exist in a constant fear or frustration or anxiety but rather that we have desires for holiness and purity, longings to feel quiet confidence before God.
>
> To push ourselves beyond the mark is, in a strange sort of way, a statement that we fear we must do the job ourselves if we expect to get it done.
>
> Balance. That is the key. I have come to sense the need to balance a type of "divine discontent"—a healthy longing to improve—with what Nephi called a "perfect brightness of hope" (2 Nephi 31:20), the Spirit-given assurance that in and through Jesus Christ we are going to make it.[23]

---

22   "Evening Balm and Morning Manna: Daily Gifts of Healing Grace," *Women in the Covenant of Grace* (Salt Lake City: Shadow Mountain, 1994), 268; emphasis added.

23   *Grace Works*, 132–33.

Endurance and Triumph

The scriptures teach that "unless a man shall endure to the end, in following the example of the Son of the living God, he cannot be saved,"[24] "but he that shall endure unto the end, the same shall be saved."[25]

Many years ago, I had the privilege of listening to President Marion G. Romney speak in general conference. President Romney had served long and faithfully as a counselor to President Spencer W. Kimball and was growing very old. I don't remember what President Romney's topic was for this particular talk, but I do remember feeling a wonderful and warm spirit emanating from him. As I listened, a great admiration for this faithful and righteous man arose within me.

At the end of his talk, President Romney must have departed from his prepared remarks because I have not been able to find his words recorded in the reports of general conference. He said simply and seriously, "I hope I can endure to the end."

His words struck me hard. If a very old and holy man who had spent a lifetime in committed service to the Lord was still occupied with enduring to the end, I needed to be far more concerned about doing so myself. Apparently, this commandment could never be mastered to the point of complete success in this life. Enduring to the end remained a challenge to President Romney. There is no box next to "Endure to the End" that we can check and be done with that task while we still live.

We can fulfill many of the essential requirements to receive eternal life very quickly. A person can be baptized in about ten seconds. The essential portion of a confirmation, being confirmed a member of the Church and receiving the gift of Holy Ghost, similarly takes only seconds. We receive our temple endowments in less than two hours. While the temple sealer may provide additional words of advice and counsel, the necessary ordinance that seals a husband and wife together for eternity is completed in less than a couple of minutes.

Two of the requirements for eternal life, however, take longer— keeping the commandments and faithfully enduring to the end.

24   2 Ne. 31:16.
25   Matt. 24:13.

Keeping the commandments is, I believe, a requirement that extends back before the beginning of our mortal life and will continue after it ends.

Enduring to the end seems much more like a constraint that applies to fallen men and women in a fallen world. This commandment relates to a period of time, earth time, which comes to a conclusion. I doubt that enduring to the end would have meaning to an immortal being in an eternal world since for him or her, there is no end.

If we were to take all of the requirements necessary for us to successfully complete our time here on this earth and plot them on a time line according to the amount of time it takes to accomplish each, we would see tiny little marks for baptism and temple ordinances and then a long, long section representing enduring to the end of our mortal lives. Almost everything discussed in this book happens during the enduring part. It is during that long journey of enduring that we must turn again and again to our Savior and His Atonement.

What does it mean to endure to the end? Are we to dig some sort of spiritual foxhole, jump in, and keep our head down until our mortal life closes? Is the best way of enduring to lock ourselves into a room, away from temptation, and wait to die?

As an emeritus member of the Seventy, Elder Robert L. Backman said,

> There is no retirement from the service of the Lord. We believe in eternal progression. We should continually grow spiritually throughout our lives. The gospel challenges us to endure to the end.
>
> The word *endure* has an interesting connotation. We seem to equate it with suffering. I was interested to discover that *endure* comes from the Latin word *indurare,* which means "to harden, to steel, make lasting." I like one of the definitions of the word *endure* found in the *Random House Dictionary.* It defines *endure* as "to have or gain continued or lasting acknowledgment or recognition, as of worth, merit, or greatness."

> When I think of the supernal joy I have experienced during my ministry, I hope those rich spiritual adventures are not ended. I know they will not be if I accept the opportunities to serve that lie ahead.[26]

So as we move forward with our lives through a fallen world, as we endure to the end of those lives, the enabling and strengthening power of the Atonement will permit us to continue to progress and grow. Elder Backman suggests that, properly understood, endurance includes its own joys and carries its own reward. With the help of the Lord, each step, each day, we will move upward, even if only a little, increasing in worth, merit, and greatness.

President Howard W. Hunter said, "Whatever Jesus lays his hands upon lives. If Jesus lays his hands upon a marriage, it lives. If he is allowed to lay his hands on the family, it lives."[27] I would humbly add, if Jesus lays his hands upon your heart, it lives and will live forever. We believe in that Jesus.

Because of that belief, we keep putting on our cardboard wings and jumping, striving to rise up to a better place, a place where that better person who lives inside us can step out from within the mortal being who has so many shortcomings and seems so ordinary. We jump, and we fall. We jump, and we fall, pulled back to earth by forces we cannot overcome.

At some time in the future, we will understand that it is time to put on our cardboard wings again. We will understand that it is time for us to jump another time. We will jump, and we will begin to fall. Then Jesus will catch us and take us a million, million, million miles back to our Heavenly Father.

We will be barred from entry to that place where we most wish to go. Then Jesus will say, "He's with me. She's with me. See, look upon the heart. Do you see the name written there? It is my name."[28]

Then we will hear the words, "Let her enter. Let him enter." And we'll put down our cardboard wings forever.

---

26 "The Golden Years," *Ensign,* Nov. 1992, 14; emphasis in original.

27 "Reading the Scriptures," *Ensign,* Nov. 1979, 65.

28 See Mosiah 5:12.

And now, behold, if Adam had not
transgressed he would not have fallen, but he would
have remained in the garden of Eden. And all things which were
created must have remained in the same state in which
they were after they were created; and they must
have remained forever, and had no end.

And they would have had no children;
wherefore they would have remained in a state of innocence,
having no joy, for they knew no misery; doing no good,
for they knew no sin.

But behold, all things
have been done in the wisdom of him
who knoweth all things.

Adam fell that men might be; and
men are, that they might have joy.

And the Messiah cometh in the
fulness of time, that he may redeem the children
of men from the fall. And because that they are redeemed
from the fall they have become free forever, knowing good from evil;
to act for themselves and not to be acted upon, save it be
by the punishment of the law at the great and last
day, according to the commandments which
God hath given.

—2 Nephi 2:22–26

"I STAND ALL AMAZED"

I stand all amazed at the love Jesus offers me,
Confused at the grace that so fully he proffers me.
I tremble to know that for me he was crucified—
That for me, a sinner, he suffered, he bled, and died.

—"I Stand All Amazed," *Hymns,* no. 193

Now the greatest and most important single thing there is in all
eternity—the thing that transcends all others since the time of the creation
of man and of the worlds—is the fact of the atoning sacrifice of Christ
the Lord. He came into the world to live and to die—to live the perfect
life and be the pattern, the similitude, the prototype for all men, and to
crown his ministry in death, in the working out of the infinite and eternal
atoning sacrifice. And by virtue of this atonement, all things pertaining to
life and immortality, to existence, to glory and salvation, to honor and
rewards hereafter, all things are given full force and efficacy and virtue.
The Atonement is the central thing in the whole gospel system.

—Elder Bruce R. McConkie, Sermons and Writings of Bruce R. McKonkie,
comp. Mark L. McKonkie (Salt Lake City: Bookcraft, 1989), 40

AFTER completing my manuscript for this book, submitting it for publication, reviewing comments and rewriting it, I decided that a concluding chapter was necessary and, I hope, beneficial.

The Atonement is a topic that does not end. The Atonement itself is infinite and eternal, and the effects of the Atonement on our lives can be infinite and eternal.[1] The ways in which the atoning sacrifice of our Savior blesses us are as numerous as all of the people who ever have lived or ever will live on this earth or any of the other worlds God has created and that Christ has saved.

As I rewrote these chapters, I was struck by how many other Atonement chapters there are yet to be written.

In the past few months, I have had the privilege of serving as a temple ordinance worker, and my increased understanding of the great work that takes place within temple walls would provide much material for a chapter entitled, "Temple Blessings and the Atonement." Many of the beloved former members of my student ward have married, and I would like to write chapters entitled, "Marriage and the Atonement" and "Your Children and the Atonement" that might assist them.

This book has touched upon the great Atonement sermons given by the prophets of the ancient scriptures. With my ever-growing appreciation for the Atonement is an ever-growing appreciation for ancient prophets who have helped me understand the Atonement, and there are many more possible chapters about their inspired insights.

Even more important is the flood of revelation we continue to receive about the Atonement from our modern prophets. On the Church's website, I searched for the number of mentions of the term "atonement" in general conference addresses over recent five-year periods of time. This is what I found:

    1995–1999—26 mentions
    2000–2004—107 mentions
    2005–2009—186 mentions

In the most recent two years prior to completion of this chapter, 2008–09, we have been taught by members of the First Presidency and Quorum of the Twelve how the Atonement is connected with the following topics, among many others:

---

1   See Alma 34:10.

- *Missionary Work and the Atonement*—Elder L. Tom Perry tells about helping investigators have faith in Jesus Christ and His Atonement.[2]
- *Healing the Consequences of Abuse and the Atonement*—Elder Richard G. Scott speaks of how the Atonement can heal both the abused and the abuser.[3]
- *Celestial Marriage and the Atonement*—Elder Russell M. Nelson explains that the Atonement makes eternal life possible through temple marriage.[4]
- *Hope and the Atonement*—President Dieter F. Uchtdorf reminds us that the Atonement is the basis for our hope for eternal life.[5]
- *Adversity and the Atonement*—President Henry B. Eyring provides assurance that our understanding of our Savior's sufferings lets us have confidence that He knows how to heal us.[6]
- *Enduring All Things and the Atonement*—President Thomas S. Monson gives us a heart-wrenching account of the terrible difficulties encountered by a Latter-day Saint woman making her way as a refugee across war-torn Europe following World War II and how her faith in the atoning sacrifice of Christ and His ability to provide her an eternal reunion with her lost family gave her strength to endure.[7]

The greatest work of Christ is centered upon His Atonement. So long as there is anyone in pain, His work will continue. So long as there is anyone suffering under the burden of sin, His work will continue. So long as there is anyone who is afraid or lonely, His work will continue. So long as there is anyone who sorrows, His work will continue. So long as there is anyone who has been faithful and who needs to be lifted up and brought back to their Heavenly Father, His work will continue.

The Atonement is infinite and eternal, and its impact on our lives can be infinite and eternal if we will turn to our Savior and follow

---

2   "The Gospel of Jesus Christ," *Ensign,* May 2008, 44–46.

3   "To Heal the Shattering Consequences of Abuse," *Ensign,* May 2008, 40–43.

4   "Celestial Marriage," *Ensign,* Nov. 2008, 92–95.

5   "The Infinite Power of Hope," *Ensign,* Nov. 2008, 21–24.

6   "Adversity," *Ensign,* May 2009, 23–27.

7   "Be of Good Cheer," *Ensign,* May 2009, 89–92.

Him. Wherever we are at the present time, wherever strange paths have taken us, if we turn toward Him, give Him our hearts, and follow Him, He will lead us out of darkness and into light. He will lead us home.

> *When He says to the poor in spirit,*
> *"Come unto me," He means He knows the*
> *way out and He knows the way up. He knows it*
> *because He has walked it. He knows the*
> *way because He is the way.*

— Jeffrey R. Holland, "Broken Things to Mend," *Ensign,* May 2006, 69–71; emphasis in original